HOW TO
HANDLE
DEPRESSION
AND LIVE
HAPPILY

HOW TO HANDLE DEPRESSION

AND LIVE HAPPILY

PRACTICAL APPROACH WITHOUT MEDICATION

Raphael T. Ikedi

authorHOUSE®

AuthorHouse™
1663 Liberty Drive
Bloomington, IN 47403
www.authorhouse.com
Phone: 1-800-839-8640

Published by AuthorHouse   09/11/2012

ISBN: 978-1-4772-2999-6 (sc)
ISBN: 978-1-4772-2998-9 (e)

CONTENTS

DEDICATION

This book is dedicated to the memory of a lady of inestimable value, who gave meaning to my life—my mom,

Late Mrs. Juliana A. Ikedi

ACKNOWLEDGMENT

My greatest appreciation and reverence goes to Almighty God who is the spiritual author of this book, I am only but a pencil in His hands. Oh God, may your throne be highly exalted forever.

I can't forget the lady of inestimable value who gave meaning to my life—my late mom. I love you mom, and will forever be proud of you. Thanks to my father whose actions made me a man.

Thanks to my siblings and in-laws, I love you dearly.

I am deeply indebted to the couple, Barr. & Mrs. Charles Ohaja who painstakingly proof-read this work—I love you. May the good Lord bless you; may he enlarge your coast and sustain you in all your endeavours.

To all my friends, the publisher and everyone that has contributed in one way or the other to my life and to the success of this book, I say a big thank you, and may the good Lord bless you all.

INTRODUCTION

Depression is a global burden which seriously reduces quality of life, for individuals and their families. It is a risk factor for suicide, self-mutilation and other physical health problems. The World Health Organization predicts that by 2020, depression will be the greatest burden of illness after heart disease. This prediction means that depression will be rampant and cause more worry in future years. This prediction is not far-fetched in our society, because of its common evidences in our individual lives. Unfortunately, depression is not openly spoken in African society, but it is pervasive. Depression affects many of us; in fact, no full-fledged man will deny the experience at one time or the other in his natural life. But the issue is the approach in handling it which goes a long way in determining the resultant effect. This book centres on practical approach without medication in handling depression.

Moreover, this book is for everyone, precisely for those who have suffered depression; those who are suffering depression; those who want to keep depression at bay; and those who have depressed people around them. It captures the true life experiences of depressed people we have in our society today; the level of decimation depression can cause in our lives if not handled in a healthy way. However, this book proffers a-way-out for this disorder and for those who have been struggling to find a meaning for their lives but failed. It is also for many people who see themselves as less human and those who have contemplated suicide or self-mutilation as a respite to hard times. By His Grace, I hope that this book will offer help, hope, assurance and usher into a long-awaited happiness to those who suffer every day in the cause of this mental disorder.

Chapter One gives a detailed definition of depression and what it does to our lives. It also brings to book some true life experiences of depression in our society. While Chapter Two chronicles the possible causes of depression in Africa—these are my experiences, what I witnessed and experiences other people have shared with me. Road to recovery is also treated in this chapter i.e. the plan to the 'promised land'. Chapter Three is on how to handle depression: practical suggestions that discourage the use of medication, while consolidating on the overlooked practices that will help us handle depression effectively. The following is Chapter Four, and it centres on the agents of happiness—things that create room for happiness like giving, honesty, optimism, etc.

Besides, Chapter Five is on food and fitness which plays a vital role in handling depression. It also captures the calming acupuncture treatment effect and spa treatment—whirlpool bath. Chapter Six is on the spiritual 'back-up' in handling depression. This chapter expects you to back-up your practical approach with prayers; not neglecting the fundamental.

The last but one chapter is termed 'For the Concerned', it is addressed to people who are concerned and should be taken seriously irrespective of age or social status. These are ways of freedom for those who are deeply entrenched by depression, those who will like to avoid it in the near future and those who will help others beat depression; everybody has a stake. The last but not the least chapter centres on what I termed 'comfort zone'—finding out what tickles you and indulging in it, no matter how funny or childish it might look. Also, this chapter outlined things to beware of in living your individual live in order to keep depression at bay.

Whether you read one chapter in its entirety every day, or read them at different paces, my earnest prayer is for this book to touch every nook and cranny of your life that may have been in the dark.

CHAPTER ONE

DEPRESSION AND WHAT IT DOES TO OUR LIVES

Depression is derived from the Latin verb 'de`primere' meaning 'to press down'. The World English Dictionary defines it as 'low in spirit; downcast; despondent. Also: distress characterised by relative economic hardship, such as unemployment.' This means that depression can be caused by anything, in the sense that, whatever gives happiness can as well cause depression.

Medically, depression is believed to be caused by chemical imbalance in the brain. Besides, our daily experiences of depression and what it actually feels like is that a dark cloud has settled on the soul. This is a stubborn feeling and it can drive a person to despair. Depression defiles our very essence and darkens our vision. It opens a gateway for satanic infusion and evil thoughts. It defecates on the soul and accuses it of being dirty and smelly. At this stage, the soul seeks no other remedy than destruction.

Depression usually catches us off guard to the extent that we no longer take cognizance of our own potentials. We only see the bad side of us. It deposits inferior thoughts in us like, 'you are stupid', 'good for nothing fool', 'idiot', 'not man enough', etc. in order to make us see ourselves as failures. Depression goes ahead to poison our minds into cynicism: seeing only the negative sides of situations. It demeans us, so that we cannot lift our heads high enough to see that we have true values in this life.

However, depression makes us unable to give in to close relationships, because we become absent in the company of those we love. We care less about ourselves: how we look, or we overdo it when we act as mask and laughing stock to the world by putting on outfits that do not give us good fit. We stumble through the way trying to find some meaning to feelings that ravage us. We lose the motivation to pursue our true vocation in life, thereby compromising our souls.

We become victims carried away by the winds of life whenever depression sets in. It makes it difficult for us to grasp on anything solid to pull ourselves together. This makes us to see only the unfairness, partiality on the side of our creator. We descend to self-loathing and pity, believing we deserve nothing better in life. We lose our sense of reasoning which results to failure of objective scrutiny of circumstances; failure to address the fact and what is fiction.

Nevertheless, let us not be drifted away by the unrealistic 'fiction' that depression is only for poor people. Depression cut across all the social strata which leave no class exempted. Many 'successful people' are on the run—running away from their own depression and trying to escape the darkness by making enough money or becoming well known, so that the trapping of fame will cushion them from their distress. But the truth is that the pain is there and except it is severely dealt with, it will remain 'a bee on the scrotum.' There is this conventional believe that 'when I get there, then I will be happy.' But I have found out that we never arrive.

Consequently, depression does not keep us at a place; we either get better or worse. One common symptom of depression is mood swings. We can go from feeling ecstatic now to feeling suicidal the next minute. It swings us like a year-old-baby who does not know what is right or wrong. It masters our minds to the point that it can change us at will. That is why, when good things happen to our neighbours or friends, we are happy with them, but once depression sees that we are happy, it will bring our woes to sadden us up.

I can remember vividly, how depression dealt with me when I was seeking for admission. Those days, I did stay in my elder brother's studio and assisted him in studio and outside work. My folks did come around to chat and while away time with me. We did all sorts of things to hide away from this menacing feeling that devastates the soul (hitting me most) such as; table tennis, draft, etc.

At the middle of all the above activities, my 'reminder' (depression) will engulf me. It will remind me that I was not supposed to be there at that time in my life. It will remind me of so many other Senior Prefects (S.Ps) like me who have gotten admission into 'Prestigious Nigerian Universities while I am here playing table tennis; even as emeritus Senior Prefect, yet a shameless fool who couldn't secure admission into any school.' For the rest of the day, I will remain despondent. Then, only the thoughts of death will occupy my mind as a respite to this pain.

The kind of depression I had those days was a constant one that never gave me breathing space. It never allowed me to see anything good about myself. Anger always occupied my mind and I could not hide it, because I was aggressive to anyone who steps on my toes. I felt shame and guilt. I felt my sole raison deter has been denied me. Depression presented the darkest side of life to me, which made it difficult for me to see the other side of the coin. It was so bad that I even said, 'God does not love me.' Depression was out to destroy me, but thank God, He led me to the antidote which led to the development of this work.

In our individual lives, we face depression in one way or the other. No man (in generic sense) will say he has never experienced it, but the question is: how do you handle yours? There are many ways to tackle depression which can help us move forward, and that is the practical approach (without medication) I am suggesting in this book. To turn around and face it head on. This will go a long way in helping us to resonate from downcast life.

This psychological condition which affects millions of people globally is as old as mankind. It poses a serious threat to our health due to the fact that it can cause even more damage than chronic diseases like hypertension or diabetes. In Africa, precisely West Africa, people suffer from different kinds of depression: financial incapacity, childlessness, unemployment, lack of electricity, loss of loved ones, break-up in relationships, lately bomb threats, unfavourable government policies, etc. Depression has no exception, children, teenagers and adults, all get a taste of it. Because of the circumstances around us, we no longer summon courage to deal with depression so that it will flee as the Holy book says 'Resist the devil, and he will flee from you' (James 4:7b KJV).

Symptoms of Depression

Anger, behaving violently, hatred, mood swings, insomnia, cynicism, bad breath, use of abusive words, being obsessive about sex, losing all interest in sex, drug and alcoholic abuse, chain smoking, inability to do anything worthwhile, harming oneself, feeling stuck, feeling isolated, malice, inconsiderate, rage, feeling stupid, feeling dead, inability to control negative thoughts, incessant loss of appetite, guilt and shame, etc.

TRUE LIFE EXPERIENCES OF DEPRESSION

Depression is a cancer that has eaten deep into the souls of our body and has set us on nothing but destruction. It seeks no permission just like death, before coming into our lives. Anybody can be a victim of this ravaging feeling: NO EXEMPTION.

Here are examples:

SEX WITH THE MOTHER

My mom used to say those days we were younger that: 'There is no clemency for anyone who has sex with his mother.' I never knew the meaning then, until this incident happened. Two boys were asked to take turns in laying with their mother in Lagos, Nigeria, by armed robbers who attacked their home. When the first son refused to do as they commanded, they shot at him, and he died.

Pointing a gun at the second son, the mother beckoned him to come, by opening her legs to eschew losing her two sons at the same time. They did it, while the armed robbers watched and laughed. Some days later, after the incident, the boy ran away from the house because he was depressed and did not know where to start in handling the pain. Till date, no one knows his whereabouts.

SUICIDE CASE

A man committed suicide last two weeks in his sitting room in Lagos. On the table where he hung, a note was discovered, and he wrote that why he killed himself was as a result of depression he'd had all his life. That something had been ravaging him for years and he couldn't bear it any longer. So, he ended the whole mess by taking his life with his hands. No wonder Aristotle said: '. . . to die in order to avoid the pains of poverty, love or anything that is disagreeable, is not part of a brave man, but of a coward.'

INFECTION

I have a cousin who was once depressed for years of what he knew nothing about. This boy suffered pains, anguish, dejection and frustration for matching on something. He was infected with cancer of the leg, what Igbo people call 'enyi' which is usually contracted by matching on the substance where it is deposited. It is an infection that eats deep into the body and damages the skin drastically. This infection on his leg reoccurs every year after treatment. Most of the treatment given to him in order to heal it permanently all proved abortive. His pocket was drained in the cause of this. He became depressed and saw no essence of his existence. He told me several times: 'My death is better than my life. What I am living is no longer life, rather I have turned into a walking corpse.' This is a depression someone causes his brother unnecessarily.

DISAPPOINTMENT

In affiliation with what Thomas Hardy said, 'A sudden disappointment of hope leaves a scar which ultimate fulfilment of that hope never entirely removes', one man got a disappointment which cost lives. This man by name, Emeka from Awka, Anambra state, went to Germany (2006) in search of greener pasture. When he got there, he did all kinds of odd jobs to make both ends meet. So he thought it wise to send down to Nigeria any tangible money he made over there to his sister, Amaka to save in the bank until he returns. He sent money to her for three consecutive years, and on the fourth year he had immigration problem which led to his repatriation.

Back in the country, he encouraged himself with the proverbial saying of a lizard that fell from Iroko tree: 'I will praise myself if no one deems it fit to do so, for it is only a strong man that falls from Iroko tree and walks on.' This he said believing he smiles to the bank after all. When he asked his sister about the money, she couldn't give him any clear cut answer because she had been lavishing the money on the man that promised her marriage. This depressed the man and not knowing how to handle it, he sought for destruction. One early morning, precisely one month after he came back, he called out his sister, after greeting her, shot her as well as him.

A MAN BUTCHERED HIS BROTHER-IN-LAW

At Omiyale Street Ejigbo, Lagos, a man butchered his brother-in-law after inviting him for a dinner, like a cow in the slaughter house. He cut him bit-by-bit, and was caught dumping the parts into a waste bin at Jakande. The reason was the rage he had over his in-law being in control of their combined business, also frustration of not owning a business at his age.

It was later gathered from his sister, (whose husband was murdered in cold blood) that the Mercedes 190 car the brother uses was given to him by her late husband. Not only that, the traditional marriage the brother had two months before the incident was sponsored by her husband. 'So, why will my brother make me a widow?' she asked. But the reason is depression.

A MAN TURNED TERRORIST DUE TO OVERWEIGHT

A man reportedly turned a terrorist due to overweight. His size shamed him, together with jokes from people. He felt he does not belong to human race: always sad, aggressive, harming himself, seeking out things that could be used for suicide. According to him, the worst years of his life where between 2006 and 2009, although he had struggled with it hitherto. He stayed depressed while his mates socialized: 'I was invited to occasions, but within this period of time I wasn't, because my presence eats up happiness,' he said. Depression dealt with him like an out-cast. The only friend he had, a girl, was epileptic—his depression got to the highest level when she jilted him.

Apparently, he joined terrorist group as a respite to end his life together with others who had made jest of him. Here is the conversation between him and the interviewer.

Interviewer: What is your name?

Member: Ahmed

Interviewer: Can you please tell us why you chose this part even when your life is at stake?

Member: Why will I live? (Interrogatory)

'HIT AND RUN' EXPERIENCE

There was a lady I met in Ondo State, Nigeria where I did my youth service, who is a good example of people that have suffered depression. This lady, by name, Nike is from a very wealthy family, but she had a problem of 'hit and run' on several occasions from men which resulted to her depression. The experience ravaged her to the level that she had no regard for anybody. She was always aggressive, arrogant and saucy to anyone who comes her way without minding the status. Many people: old and young, complained the uncultured manner she displayed, even to strangers. Accidentally, our parts crossed on the day of our endurance trek. She had a puncture and we happened to be at the scene. While trying to help her out, she still exhibited those characteristics of a depressed person. That pissed my friend, and he left. On my own part, I utilized the opportunity to know actually the reason behind her mannerism, and not necessarily for helping sake.

In the cause of helping her, she let the cat out of the bag. According to her, she'd had countless number of fiancé who leaked her body as well as her purse. For her, she had done her best to have a good relationship: prayed, fasted, and consulted many men of God and specialists, all to no avail. She asked me: 'Why are there no good men in the world? Why am I always left shattered to pick the pieces of my life?' After which, she went into her car without a thank you. The last word I heard from her before she zoomed off was, 'I have turned my back against the world.'

A MAN STABBED HIS BANKER WIFE TO DEATH

In June, 2011 a man was reported to have stabbed his banker wife to death and locked her inside the room, probably hoping no one will find out. Fortunately, when the lady did not show up in the office after some days the police got involved and caught him.

What led to this ungodly action? The man was jobless at that material moment while the wife was still gainfully employed. His joblessness led to frustration which transmuted into depression; his incapability made his wife the bread winner of the family. Instead of channelling his thoughts to neutral-thinking, he went for destruction. He thought negatively, just like the Holy Book says, 'For as a man thinket in his heart so is he . . .' (Pro.23:7a KJV)

A LADY WHO WANTED TO JUMP INTO THE RIVER

A woman was caught at third mainland bridge Lagos, trying to jump into the river. When asked by the people who intervened in her suicidal mission, after they had pleaded for several minutes, she opened up and I quote:

> 'You people are wicked by stopping me
> What is life after all? When no one care
> about you, when you have to bear your
> pains and wipe your tears . . .'

After the incident, we gathered that this lady had a master's degree, but nepotism and some unforeseen forces made her unable to secure any job for the past five years. In addition, she was not married which was one of the catalysts that aggravated her misery.

THE MAN THAT LOST HIS WIFE TO A WEALTHY GUY

This suicidal mission also took place in third mainland bridge. A motorcyclist, 'okada man' as popularly called, accidentally hit the back bomber of a saloon car. When the woman inside the car came out, after inspecting her car insisted the 'okada man' must repair it. Before you can say J A C K, the man held the woman and jumped together with her into the water. By the time the divers who were not on sight when this happened got to them, they were both dead. It was later discovered that the man had a depression of losing his wife to a wealthy guy; though he attempted suicide hitherto, but for neighbour's intervention. So when this opportunity came up, he utilised it to end his life together with the woman's.

RAPE INCIDENCE

In Enugu, a man watched as some group of guys raped his wife on the night of their honey-moon. This happened at night of their wedding, as they were about to start their lives as husband and wife, a group of masked gunmen barged into their matrimonial room and requested for nothing but to have sex with the woman while the husband watched.

At the initial stage, the couple offered them the money they realised from the wedding, but the sons of the devil declined. Before they could increase the amount to five million, they launched an attack on the man, after hitting him, forced him to watch as the three guys took turns in lying with the wife. Not only that they raped her but also deflowered her in the husband's presence. After the incident, the couple became depressed to the extent they divorced shortly afterwards.

These and many more are examples of life experiences of depression we find within our neighbourhood. What it means is that, cases of depression in our society today are alarming, and the earlier we realise it the better for all of us.

CHAPTER TWO

CAUSES OF DEPRESSION

In this chapter, we are not looking at medical technicalities of causes of depression, rather the practical and everyday experiences that induce depression in our day-to-day activities.

This two-syllabic word 'de-press' denotes that something is being pushed down. It suggests that something is no longer where it used to be; it has been tampered with. We are depressed because we have pushed down emotions that we cannot allow to the surface. We constantly experience a range of emotions, and how we handle them determines the level of our mental health. If we feel angry and do not express the anger in a healthy way, we will either act it out in a way that is detrimental to us or push it down which becomes depression. When we feel sorrow but do not let it out, we hold back the tears until they are too 'pressed down' to be released. We all face adversity in our lives, but how we respond to it is the direct response to the way we have been taught to react.

Most causes of depression are as a result of past experiences or encounters we had. Biologically, our personalities are moulded in the first six years of our lives and it is the quality of care we receive in our early years that makes us what we are. Also, it determines our choice of friends and lovers, shapes our interests, and determines our careers; even changes our brain pattern and body chemistry. It also triggers mental illness, including depression, bad breath or criminal behaviours later on in life.

Here are some of the scenarios that can induce us into despair when we do not have tools for counselling ourselves.

LOSS OF SOMEONE CLOSE TO US

The death of someone dear to us can be depressing. This is absolutely human nature. Even though it is highly personal the way we handle the cases, but there are elements of similarity. I have been a victim of losing someone I loved so much. So I know exactly what it feels like: 'He who feels it knows it' (Chinua Achebe).

Permit me to share my experience with you. When I heard the news of my mum's death, it was as if I was floating without a destination. I experienced what I can call a 'dark cloud barricaded with a thick coat, one made of heavy fabric, and I was stuck in it with no means of escape.' The depression of losing her poisoned my mind and I became dejected, despondent, etc. Sadness became a food for my thought. I couldn't see anything good in everything because what warms me up was sorrow. But it wasn't constant this time around because I had started acquiring the techniques of handling depression. So, this is one of the cases that keep us depressed for years if not handled in a healthy way, this is in connection with the words of John Carson, 'When you lose someone you love, you die too and you wait around for your body to catch up.'

PAST ABUSE

Past abuse is one of the major causes of depression. It could be a past physical, sexual, emotional abuse, etc. It is a clear evidence that most of the people who have been abused in the past, greater number of them, suffer depression. One of my classmates in primary school days was sexually abused by her uncle when we were in primary six and for all I could remember, I only saw her brooding all the time.

FEELING OF HAVING NO CONTROL

This can occur when we try to control other people and the result turns out to be negative. Attempting to change another person only leads to frustration and disappointment. It can be seen in our intimate relationships, at work, with our siblings, with our children, in dealing with our parents or with friends. This is an unexpressed frustration and disappointment at others not behaving as we want, which can easily lead to depression.

INCAPACITY

Depression can set in if our body has let us down through illness or old age. People who found themselves disabled often get depressed, because they believe they cannot function like other people. This is also prevalent in the elderly people whose physical bodies cannot move them around as they used to. Feeling physically helpless can be one of the major causes of depression and helplessness.

In addition, those that surfer venereal diseases and terminal diseases are often depressed. They believe that their lives have come to an end due to the way the case was presented to them, and stigmatization that accompanies it. Most times they seek no other remedy than destruction.

IN A DEAD END OF RELATIONSHIP

We may be in a relationship we can't simply see a way out. At this stage we may feel trapped by the circumstances and have fallen into the belief that we cannot move away from the situation. This actually poses more problems when we think that our partner is indispensable due to his or her financial assistance. At this juncture, we realize that the relationship is the root cause of our misery, yet we are stuck. We are at this point dependent personalities who are terrified of abandonment and willing to do anything to hold on to the relationship.

Some of us, after putting all the efforts, time, sacrifices and commitment in a relationship our partner pays us back by jilting us. We remain depressed, oblivious of the fact that: 'you do not get a better view of masquerade standing at one spot.'

POWERLESSNESS

When we feel powerless, a gate has been opened for depression to come in. This usually happens when we allow someone else to dictate for us as if we are children. We feel powerless even to make our own decision from the suggestions people give us. I can still recall what my mom told me, she said: 'Son, one can only advice you; you take the decision yourself. 'So, as adults, if we don't take decisions ourselves, we may feel bullied, violated by others and feel that we are in hopeless situations.

LACK OF FINANCE

Lack of finance is one of the major causes of depression. Imagine when a man does not have money to shave his beard or buy a small unit of airtime; it leaves him with nothing else than depression. This easily occurs when a man finds it difficult or 'impossible' to take care of his basic needs. The next thing that will come to his mind is negative thoughts. He turns his mind away from positive thinking or neutral thinking, rather channelling it into 'black and white thinking', rage, anger and frustration. We at this point push it further by transferring the aggression on others, thereby lashing and blaming them for our misfortune.

POST-NATAL DEPRESSION

There is a conjecture about why women become depressed after giving birth. Medical papers are devoted to theorizing on post-natal depression and the role hormonal change plays. Notwithstanding, there are very simple explanations for it (based on the research I carried out on post-natal women): being physically shattered; the overwhelming responsibility of caring for the baby; a feeling of isolation; giving up on what drops coin into the pocket due to maternity (it feels good to make your own money, you know); loss of the pretty look of a lass. When these happen the last thing a post-natal mother wants is to take care of the baby, regardless of how much she adores it. But she feels she has no choice which will keep her depressed the more.

RETIREMENT

Retirement can be tiresome, especially when we have spent years being busy. At this time, whatever we have been running away from catches us when we stop. We feel at this juncture that we are no longer needed. We feel that the society has used and dumped us. It can seem like our raison deter has gone, thereby depression occupies the soul. Brendan Frances felt this way when he said: 'At inner most core of all loneliness is a deep and powerful yearning for union with one's lost self.'

INFERIORITY COMPLEX

Without mincing words, many of us are depressed because we believe we are below the standard. This can easily be seen amongst us when we think that our mates have better physical qualities than we do. Examples of these are when we think we are brief, plain, skinny, not fine, below financial measurement, etc. It does not end there, we carry on with the impression that people do not like us: too bad to be admired. We may feel people greet our friends more than they do us and we feel intimidated. One of my school mates once told me:

> Mate: 'Raph! I don't like walking
> with you.'

> Me: 'May I know why, please?'

Mate: 'You greet so many people
and none knows me.'

Me: 'Why are you perturbed?'

Mate: 'You intimidate me.'

On hearing the above statement, I laughed my heart out; because that was the first time I heard something like that. Hitherto, I never knew or believed that someone can feel such way. But now I know; that can really cause depression and for the purpose of this book it will be addressed.

COMPETING WITH EVERYONE

In this contemporary world, it is not gainsaying the fact that everyone is a competitor. No one wants to be identified as a failure. Due to this, we always feel a vacuum inside us that we will never be good enough. We are often confronted with ideas, images and stories about how we should live our lives. Icons are held up as examples of what we should achieve. Stories of others are pasted on the walls of the streets we walk, on television, national dailies and internet, so that we have no option than strive to get to the height others have reached—believing that happiness will come when we get there.

Moreover, this competitive spirit propels us to set unrealistic goals. A goal that based on what we do at the material moment, even to a novice, is not achievable. At the end of the day when we fail to realize our over-blown objectives we become disappointed, and depression follows.

LOSS OF CHILDHOOD

Loss of childhood can cause a serious depression when we lack the ecstatic experiences of it. What I mean by this is childhood entitlements: full of fun and happiness; secured and a sense of belonging that we feel safe knowing full well that we are being cherished; have no worries, rather believe that things are okay. When all these are found wanting the grown-up may be feeling isolated and uneasy with others. That is why some of us find it difficult to stand up for ourselves; rather we put others before us. We fear criticism and take it as a threat. We judge ourselves harshly and have very low self-esteem.

Loss of childhood could be as a result of bad parental upbringing, environmental atmosphere, educational background, peer group mingle, societal influence, etc. The negative influence from these our past can lead to mental illness and depression. People who do not deal with their unremitting depression can run the risk of ending up in prison, mental institution or even die. But there is still hope for recovery and many have recovered.

UNEMPLOYMENT

Unemployment is one the factors that causes depression in this global village. The situation is heightened especially when someone loses his job, or when one has sent applications to so many companies yet no positive response. It rose to this stage for a man I met during my computer training period. He frankly told me one day:

> 'O boy, I am depressed. I feel frustrated. After four years of my NYSC I couldn't secure a job in any company. Not because I have not passed their interviews, but I don't know why . . .'

The issue of unemployment which is nothing to write home about is one of the leading factors of depression amongst youths, especially graduates of these days. Unemployment makes a graduate feel worthless and cages him with shame, especially after so many years without a job. At this stage, we become conformist—always interested to know what people think about us; whether they think we went to school to while away time, or if we really went to school as we claim. It is also, one of propelling factors of drug trafficking, 'yahoo scam', the use of alcoholic drinks and drugs for medication.

COMPARING OURSELVES WITH OTHERS

Comparison in a way is interwoven with competition which has been treated, but there is difference therein. In comparing ourselves with others we try to bring out similarities between ourselves and the person involved. These are the things we have in common: our age mate, school mate, colleague, etc. Comparing with others most especially 'wrong' people will only do one thing to us; DEPRESS. This is a simple but big mistake we make that has no good effect on our lives if not woes. We compare ourselves not even occasionally but on daily basis. This is usually based on the material things our mates have acquired without taking cognizance that this is a wicked world and that we have different purposes in life. We then end up with no other choice than self-pity.

DISRUPTED HOME

Disrupted home causes depression both for children and the couple involved. Children who are products of divorced or separated families, because of lack of emotional support from parents as one big family suffer depression. They always feel a vacuum in their lives, which was supposed to be filled at different levels of growth. Because of this, there is always this feeling of less-human—imagine someone calling you a bastard, simply because you are staying with only your mother or father instead of both parents, it is depressing. On the other hand, the couple who are involved feel depression which accompanies separation. The depression is usually higher for the person who feels cheated, and she or he will remain depressed for life if not handled in a healthy way.

SECURITY THREATS

Insecurity is one of the major causes of depression that affect all the social strata in our society today. People lose their lives, family members, properties and are even rendered homeless which leaves them with no other option but depression. In Africa, particularly Nigeria, people now live in perpetual fear of falling victims to the spate of bombings, assassinations, kidnappings and other acts of terrorism. The recent bombing of UN house situated in FCT, Abuja, claimed so many lives and left many frightened.

Also, the bomb attack in the headquarters of Nigerian Police Force, Abuja on 16th June,2011 to mention but a few, has taken place in recent times. The Boko Haram has taken a new deadly twist with dreaded groups issuing threats to eliminate all Christians and Muslims serving in federal government: 'This is a government that is not Islamic, so both Muslim and non-Muslim employees are considered infidels.' The members of the sect do not spare royalty or religious leadership. So, this has become a paramount issue of security threat that leads to depression.

ROAD TO RECOVERY

> "I do not feel obliged that the same God who endowed us with sense, reason and intellect has intended us to forgo their use"
>
> Chessmaster Savielly G.T

When we say road to recovery, we mean a map or a plan which will take us to the 'promised land.' In a state of depression, two things come to our mind: either to face it head on and move into recovery or to 'medicate' the feeling and avoid anguish that accompanies depression. For the purpose of this book, we use the word 'medication' to describe anything that is used to avoid feelings. Medicating can include excesses of the following; drugs, alcohol, nicotine, gambling, working, sex, eating, not eating, exercising, helping others, judging others, wickedness, etc.

Facing depression with a view to conquer it can be a hard option. That is why we easily divert to medicating the feelings as a way of not allowing ourselves to become overwhelmed with grief and pain. But we can face serious problems when the behaviour that serves to medicate depression becomes troublesome in its own right. The drugs or substances we use to medicate depression can force us to lose our jobs, damage our family relationships or friendships, and lead us to addiction and dependency. When this happens, we have another problem to address. It is at this stage that either our denial lifts or we medicate further. As I said earlier, it does not stay at a place—either better or worse.

We stop denying our problems when we feel strong enough to face them. When denial lifts, it can be very painful, but the human mind will not lift its own denial if it is not strong enough to cope with what it is trying to deny. Because the deeper the depression the stronger the denial. One thing we do not need is self-reproach for not having faced up our problems sooner.

When we medicate our emotions in order to hide away from our problems, we medicate everything. We cannot medicate our negative feelings and leave ourselves with a supply of good feelings. In medicating our depression, we also medicate the ability to feel happy, joy, excited and alive. It is all or nothing. Based on my experience and research carried out, I have come to realise that medicating anything, medicates everything.

During my depressed moments, I medicated with alcoholic drinks, unknown to me that I was medicating depression alongside my happiness. I discovered that after medicating, depression gets angrier with me and beckons on its cohorts to come over. When I took cognizance of this, I desisted from medicating and sought for the practical approach to handling depression.

For those who medicate with substances that contain nicotine like cigarette, Indian hemp, mandrake or hard drugs, we know it is hard to stop. But the reality is that if you don't look for a way to stop, it will in turn stop your life. There are steps we can take to stop medication that may not be too hard on us. We know we cannot put down this habit in one day that is why I am suggesting gradual process—begin right now by cutting down on the quantity you take. For example, if you used to smoke ten sticks of cigarette at a go, you cut it down to five, give it some weeks and cut it to three sticks, go down until you are able to overcome the addiction; the same applies to other substances. You may also involve a practitioner, friend or relative who will help you in maintaining the cutting-down strategy. Remember, denying your depression and the pain it goes with will lift and return. Recovering from depression is like peeling layers of onion. We peel one layer, then, we go on to the next one.

MILESTONE

In pursuing this course, we need to set a milestone which is an important factor to recovery. Below are the milestones you will reach if you follow the suggestions in this book.

- You can make mistakes, yet feel liberated from constant self-criticism

- Accept that your feelings are okay; they are normal human feelings.

- There is no shame in struggling; but release yourself from pursuit of perfection.

- It is okay to be honest with yourself; constantly lying complicates everything for you.

- You are entitled to want things.

- Fear is the consequence of self-judgement; as you judge yourself less, fear will diminish.

- Self-protection comes at a price; when you stop denying your pain, you open up to the gift of recovery.

- Learn to take responsibilities for your actions.

- You will feel confident enough to enjoy the fruit of intimacy.

CHAPTER THREE

HOW TO HANDLE DEPRESSION

We live in a society infused with pharmaceuticals, drugs and substances to medicate everything about depression and anxiety, but there lie in wait: addiction and dependency. Many of us believe that there is no other means to ease the symptoms but drugs and other medications. This is where we come in with the natural and practical way of handling depression without necessarily the use of drugs or medications.

When we say, how to handle depression, we simply mean ways by which we can deal with this unpleasant situation and probably improve. The suggestions given in this book are not automatic. It is a gradual process, whereby if it is properly applied will help our situations immensely, and we will live happily. This is a natural healing.

Below are the suggestions and how to apply them.

SURRENDER

> "The only way to leave is to accept each minute as an unrepeatable miracle . . ." Margaret Storms.

When we are depressed the first wise thing to do is to surrender. This is a process of accepting the status quo instead of running away: accept you have lost your loved one; accept that you have lost your job or have not been employed; accept you have been jilted in a relationship; accept that you are financially incapable; accept you have no partner, etc. But desist from using harsh words on yourself at this moment, words like 'idiot', 'good for nothing fool', 'never do well', etc. At times like this just stop, breathe in and out; you will notice a release of tension in your stomach. Accept the depression at that moment—know that you are depressed.

By accepting, you will feel a sense of relief in you. This will calm you down; also make you understand that you do not need to sort it out there and then. You can just relax and sit with the feeling of being depressed. It is not self-judgement, this is honesty. Being depressed does not mean you are going to die; it means you feel depressed.

Exercise:

Stand up

Put two of your arms in the air

⚜ Close your eyes and focus on that your pain

⚜ Concentrate for five minutes

⚜ Now say: I SURRENDER.

As you say this, with honesty, you will feel a spirit of acceptance which helps you to go to the next layer.

When I was depressed, it was my inability to accept that wore me down. Once I accepted the depression; I stopped betraying myself and sought for remedy. For some of us, our depression is not as big as they seem, but it is being scared of accepting that hydra-heads it. ACCEPT AND ENJOY THE FEELING.

FACE REALITY

"You can avoid reality, but cannot avoid the consequences of avoiding reality" Alyn Rand.

In facing reality, we should know that trying to perform when we are depressed only compounds the problem. There is no point in competing with others at this moment. Conserve your energy, and if you have the luxury of time take yourself to somewhere safe: withdraw from the world. Be honest with yourself, and give yourself the permission to take time out from trying to please others. Drop the responsibilities that do not matter. Do only those that matter like feeding yourself, working to make both ends meet, praying, etc.

Notwithstanding, the good news is that whenever you face reality, you face your worst fear. While facing your worst fear, you will grow in stamina to do it again, and your courage will automatically increase.

If you think this suggestion is not for you, then ask yourself this question: WHO AM I COMPETING AGAINST? If I will not slow down on my engagements and get back my life then, I will be faced with decreasing energy that will leave me more helpless and hopeless.

WRITE ON IT

> "The great thing to be recorded is the state of your own mind . . . write immediately while the impression is fresh, for it will not be the same a week afterwards"
>
> Samuel Johnson,1773.

One of the ways to handle depression is to write down on paper how you feel. Write the words as they flow and allow it to spell itself out on the paper. By writing, you release uncomprehending tension that has bottled up inside you. Writing down the way you feel can give you a sense of comfort and may lead to the solution for your depression. While writing, point out the things that make you feel 'guilt' and 'shame' it is very important, because these are the weapons that carry out the assignment of depression.

Here are some topics to write on:

- ❖ When did I start having this feeling?

- ❖ What triggers the reoccurrences?

- ❖ What are the roles played by others in this feeling?

- ❖ What role have I been playing for this feeling?

- ❖ What have I been trying to avoid?

- ❖ What have I benefited from this feeling?

- ❖ What should I do to stop feeling this way?

Read the work or give it to someone to read to your hearing when you have exhausted what is on your mind at the moment. Believe you me, a plausible lift of heavy thought shall you experience. These have worked for me and for many others, try it.

TALK TO YOURSELF

> "The greater amount of truth is impulsively uttered; thus the greater amount is spoken . . ."
> Edgar Allan Poe.

Some people may find this out of place but it works. Talking to oneself is one of the ways to relieve the monotony of depression. We live in a society that 'clamps down' on 'no talk' and encourages 'I am fine.' So, talking to yourself will be a good way to handle your pains. Talk as if you are in a conversation with someone and say those things that hold you hostage. After, proffer a solution as if you are responding back to a problem brought before you. Advice yourself and you will see that the antidote to the misery has been right inside of you all this while.

Another way to go about this is to make use of a recorder which could be a radio tape, videotape or even a phone that has recording facility. Once you get any of these ready (put it on record), begin to pour out your soul without restraint. Talk as if you are having a conversation with an angel. Open up whatever your pain is. Talk as long as expression is still in your mouth. When through, give it some time, play the record and listen to it. As you are listening to how you feel, remedy will come, and your pains will be lifted. Do not disregard this, give it a trial and you will see the wonder.

SHADE TEARS WHEN NECESSARY

"Grief itself is a medicine"
William Cowper, 1782

People eschew crying and shading tears when they are depressed. The reason is that they believe it will make them lose control. NO!! I totally disagree with that reason. If you begin to cry, you will stop when your essence has had enough. You will only be given what you can handle. Your mind will only expand what it deems safe to expand. This is a natural human evolution. You have to trust yourself and push forward because to release those feelings are one of the essential ways of handling depression. I advised one of my friends, who is quite older than I am, some time ago to shade tears that it will help him regain his life. But he instantly objected. One day, he gave it a trial, and it worked for him, he told me 'Raph! I never knew there is something in this your small head.' I cannot forget that statement.

DO NOT BOTTLE UP ANGER

"Anger is a great force. If you control it, it can be transmuted into a power which can move the world."
Swami Sivananda

To bottle up anger can be devastating. Anger not dealt with in childhood can grow into depression in adulthood. Childhood abuse transfers to abusive adulthood. We need to move from our childhood rage in order to develop into competent happy adults.

As children, we were not taught or encouraged to express our emotions, especially in this part of the world, and this makes us ignorant on how to release the anger. If we are angry and do not deal with it, it does not go away, rather it accumulates inside us. Here are the signs of bottled-up anger: sarcasm, nightmare, smiling when you don't want to, becoming irritated at irrelevant things, refusing eye contact, not sleeping or sleeping too much, inferiority complex, body tics, etc.

Are you in doubt of the above signs? No problem. Just ask anyone you can trust to tell you the truth about your reaction. Please do not be angry with the person, rather work on it for it is a path to your freedom. Many of us who have this anger from childhood to adulthood, that is so scary, should not be ashamed, rather look for a professional practitioner, a pastor or your role model to assist you in releasing the rage in a way that is not harmful to you or anyone else. Secondly, the fierce anger can be utilised for a better purpose. Divert the anger towards determination to make a change in the area that induced the anger, then, fulfilment/happiness will come.

REACHING YOUR PAIN

Pain is the feeling we have in our body when we have been hurt. In order to reach this pain, we need to let out anger as has been treated above. This is because anger is the front-end of pain. When we feel angry it ends up in pain, and it is usually a feeling of futility, hopelessness, or unfairness. In other words, pain is the 'soft tears' that lies behind anger.

There are many ways to reach your pain which could be finding a safe atmosphere for relaxation, meditation, or writing. While doing any of these, try as much as possible to be specific and honest to yourself. To really get at the pain, visualize yourself as a child: meditate, write, and relax at the beach or cool place as a child. What I mean by this is, do any of the activities like a child not as an adult would. Make sure that your reasoning and writing at this material moment portray that of a child; you may use your uncommon hand to write, which will help you reach your vulnerable spot.

While working on this, express your sadness exactly the way you feel. If not so, pain will build a duplex on the foundation it has already laid on your life. Let go of the past. The more you let out, the better you heal. Hold yourself tight and let the tears out. Letting out tears will free you from the past. Imagine tears as hard currency to purchase your healing—not weakness.

Give yourself permission to mourn for what you have lost. The more pain you release the less frightened the feelings will become. By so doing my brother and sister, you will experience a state of forgiveness for yourself and others.

Note: Do not bother if you cannot reach the pain at once, it is a gradual process. Just be open and the positive result will come.

LEARN TO SAY "NO, THANK YOU."

> "When a person acts without knowledge of what he thinks, feels, needs or wants, he does not yet have the option of choosing to act differently."—Clark Moustakas

We are depressed most times when we compromise ourselves. Many of us consent to things we do not actually want, simply because we are frightened or at the mercy of others. When we go out of our way to please others at our own expense, it may leave us empty and even in resentment of others. People have recovered from depression by simply saying, 'no thank you' when they are being asked to take on too much. We may be uncomfortable doing this for the first time if we are not accustomed to say no; because we get quilt feelings for standing up for our rights. We should bear it in mind that, it is our right to make decisions. So, when we feel uncomfortable, we should let others know our limits.

Exercise:

- Start by saying 'no' to your unwanted thoughts. Say no to those evil thoughts that go on in your mind.

- Stand in front of the mirror and say: 'No, thank you' to yourself as if you are talking to someone.

- Practice some conversation in which you compromise yourself and say, 'no, thank you.

- When you are through, just go to the person who you wish to face and do exactly what you have practiced, in a polite manner.

As an adult you are entitled to say—NO—to anything you do not wish to undertake.

When facing an authority, you should learn to be clear about your goal. Your goal needs to be about you and how you will like to feel. It needs to address what you need to get off your chest, how you want to change your behaviour in the company of others and how you want to lessen the negative effect that someone has on you. For example, you may constantly feel humiliated when a colleague talks to you as though you were a delinquent teenager. So, in order to tackle this, you need to prepare yourself to approach the whole set-up with a different mindset. Practice your preferred response in the mirror as shown above or with a close person until you get the right feeling.

DEALING WITH SHAME

> "Our discontent begins by finding false villains who we can accuse of deceiving us. Next we find false heroes who we expect to liberate us. The hardest, most discomforting discovery is each of us must emancipate himself."
>
> Daniel J. Boorstin.

When we feel discomforted and imprisoned, it is shame that binds us to our depression. Shame makes us not to be open to the world; we cannot receive from others. We do not trust ourselves not to fall apart if we talk about it, because we feel of no value. This is something we experience as children. If we feel shame, we have a hangover from the way an adult has habitually addressed us. As adults, we continue to talk to ourselves in that manner. Shame grabs our heads and pulls it down so that others can't see us. Shame leaves us believing that we are worse than anyone else. Fear of being 'found out' about how shameful we are drives our lives.

However, until the shame is confronted we are trapped. As adults, we can deal with this shame by allowing some light into our lives to kill off the shame. Shame left in the dark multiplies. So identify the things that led to your shameful feeling and deal with them. Below are some of the things that make us feel ashamed.

- We feel less than others: We simply don't feel good in the company of others no matter how many times we have been with them.

- We feel shamed because we are not gainfully employed.

- We feel shamed because we do not get encomiums from people just like our friend.

- When someone sees us cry, we feel we are weak.

- We feel we are poor and have no right to express ourselves.

- We judge ourselves harshly.

- We feel we are living in lie and do everything to keep up the lie.

- We feel we are inferior to others because of our background.

✦ We feel we are gullible etc.

As we begin to expose things that make us feel ashamed, we will feel better about ourselves.

TALK TO SOMEONE

> "Talking to someone can act as a release for our feelings"
> Alexandra Massey.

As the saying goes 'problem shared is problem solved.' Talking to someone is a good idea but the question is—who? You need to know who you are sharing your problems with. In this context, talking to someone won't help if the person is having a great life and does not know what it feels like to be in your shoes. Look for someone who knows exactly how you feel. It is only a dead body that knows what it feels like to die. For instance, you slept with a sex worker as a result of marital depression and tell the experience to your friend who is not yet married; it is obvious he will not see reasons with you.

Besides, know who you talk to and what you say in order not to implicate yourself. For example, you don't go telling an EFCC man the financial crime you committed in your darkest moments, because he will definitely not view it from the same angle.

Classification of the groups

Therapy

This is one-on-one discussion with a therapist who will help give us objective information about ourselves. With therapy, we can go back to when we stopped growing, address any trauma, retrain ourselves and then heal. A good therapy can provide the treatment required for the emergency situation of chronic depression. A good therapist can be found from recommendations of counselling authorities, like University Teaching Hospitals. When you get to any of these, ask them for their counselling departments.

Unprofessional groups

These are self-help groups that run without facilitators. This means they are free-for-all and render support amongst them. The most popular of these is 12 step groups. The organization that grew out of this initial meetings came to be known as 'Alcoholic Anonymous' or AA and it is the model subsequent 12 step groups that deal with different addictions besides alcoholism. These groups are common in developed countries like UK, US, etc, but here in Africa some NGOs now run such groups.

Facilitated groups

Take a risk and live happy: this is my advice for anyone who wants to live happy. Make out time find these groups of professional facilitators and allow others comment on the part of you that has shamed you for years. You will experience a sense of liberation as it downs on you that there is no need hiding this part of your life from others. The most exciting thing about this is that they will give you a positive response.

These groups can be found anywhere: Doctors' surgeries offer groups run by nurses for giving up smoking; Christian centres offer groups for assisting a spiritual life foundation; therapist offer groups for women who struggle in relationships; counsellors' offer counselling services on elaborate issues, etc.

CHAPTER FOUR
AGENTS OF HAPPINESS

GIVING

> "I have found that among its other benefits, giving liberates the soul of the giver" Maya Angelou.

Giving is one of the conspicuous agents that carry out the activities of happiness. It is important to assist someone in need no matter how little. Though, there are so many uncultured responses: ingratitude on the side of the needy; lives cut short after giving; collapse of business after giving and countless number of destinies being taken away after giving—still give, rather with wisdom. There is a reward of joy released in your life, especially when you give with wisdom. This means, as you sow smile into someone's life wisely, you will reap happiness.

Do you know you can generate joy in your heart as depression tries to pull you down by putting a smile on faces of the people you are better than? I have had this experience and till this day anytime I remember it I feel happy, even though it was small. As I was brooding one morning, one man who is old enough to be my uncle came to buy something from my sister's shop. We got talking and he told me his health condition, though not expecting anything from me. After which I contributed the little I had on me. To be honest with you, I became happy instantly, and any day I remember that I contributed to his life am gladdened.

Meditation

"The summary of a man's problem is his inability to be alone in the silent room" Raphael.

Meditation is one of the powerful agents of happiness. This is the act of sitting quietly, breathing deeply, focusing on the present and becoming aware of one's thoughts without judging them. Meditation helps the body to relax. Research has shown that meditation lifts mood and decreases stress when practiced daily. There is also evidence that it helps mild depression.

We can meditate in many ways, which could be use of soulful music. When we hear soulful meditative music, our inner being begins to aspire for deeper and more meaningful reality. This reality is the secret of meditation. When we are aspiring for joy or peace of mind, our soul meditates spontaneously on our behalf, which is the work of music. 'Each time we hear soulful music, we get inspiration and delight. In the twinkling of an eye, music can elevate our consciousness.' Sri Chinmoy.

Also, there is another way the activity of meditation can be carried out to ease the tension of depression. This is the one I use myself whenever the tension is high. Below is how to do it.

Exercise

- Sit or lie down comfortably

- Let your thought come and go for a minute (You will sense the feeling that your thought engender)

- Now turn your racing thought into a calm and still lake

- Visualise it as quiet and placid as a mirror

- Now feel the calmness; the surface, the beauty and stillness of the lake

- As fear rises from the surface then let it float away on the surface of the lake until it becomes calm once more.

The above is a technique that helps to combat our racing mind and help forge a space for healing. For those who have suffered in a long while, and are highly susceptible to depression, employing meditation will help a lot in keeping it at bay. At its best, meditation can help us reach a state of joy we never knew was possible.

ALL FINGERS ARE NOT EQUAL

"Until you make peace with who you are, you will never be content with what you have" Raphael.

Realising that all fingers are not equal and that everyone is given a particular assignment according to his own ability is one of the agents of happiness. Many of us fail to understand this and it ends us up in depression. We have different purposes in life so let us not be carried away by the achievements of our friends. Just be happy with them and strive to do well in your own field of assignment.

Irrespective of the sizes of the fingers, each has a specific role to play. That is why; whenever a particular task arises the one best fit will be summoned. If we can discover our ability in life, we will discover happiness. It is also pertinent to note that, because you did not succeed in a particular thing and your friend did does not make you a failure. Check yourself very well, there must be something of worth you possess that your friend does not have.

HONESTY

Honesty is one of the effective catalysts of happiness. The big part of us that is experiencing depression stems from 'make belief' and living in 'fool's paradise.' Until we learn this is not conducive to our wellbeing, we will be stuck. Some of the depression that emanate from our relationships, at the place of work, in school, in the market, are because we have made lies and lying lips our watch-word.

So many of us have lied to ourselves and to others to the extent that we no longer have our lives to ourselves, rather we have become victims of lies. It does not end there, in trying to keep up with the lies, we enslave ourselves the more. In this case complication becomes an understatement, because of the despicable damage lies can cause in our lives. Some of us may cross the Rubicon at this stage; even to deny our own blood due to lies we have surrounded ourselves with.

Lily, a girl from my faculty when we were in school complicated herself by the false life she lived, to the extent that she denied her own biological mother before the students. She created the impression that she was from a very wealthy family. She usually talks of her people: series of cars in her father's garage, how she had several maids at her service, how money was never an issue in her family, etc. She refused to associate with anybody from her home town so that people will not know her true identity.

As the Lord would have it, one day, her mom came to our school to see her after she (Lily) had not visited home for months. When this girl came out from the lecture room, and was directed to her mother waiting outside with the food stuff she brought, she practically denied never to have known anybody like that. Even when the woman called her by her native name, she ignored her and walked away.

The denial in the above incidence came because she wanted to keep up with her lies of false life. So my brothers and sisters let us do away with false lives and make beliefs; it does not pay. Try as much as you can to be honest with yourself and to others. Whatever family or condition you find yourself, try not to lie about it for God knows why He put you there. It is better not to say anything about yourself than to lie. It is also an honourable thing not to bear testimony than to bear a false one—beware. Being truthful is one the agents that carry out the activities of happiness.

'SIMPLE BUT EFFECTIVE'

> "If you can't explain it to a 6-year-old,
> you don't understand it yourself"
> Albert Einstein

One 'simple but effective' thing to do when we are depressed is to remember the child in us. Remembering the child in us is a way to be happy. When you are depressed close your eyes and remember the child in you. If you have a problem getting that vision, then get a photograph of yourself as a child. As you see yourself as a child, pay attention to your feelings; this might look awkward but give it a trial. Go to your child, become a therapist to the child by imagining what a therapist will say to a child. Explain to him that he is reacting to something that is imaginary, that no harm is going to come to him. Use your adult reasoning to bring this information to him. Practice this, until your feelings change.

Practicing this will bring some comfort usually after some minutes. If you are constant, you will find comfort on regular basis. This is because you are speaking to the core of yourself, thereby handling depression from the inside out.

This is a piece of magic and people who do this live in a state of joy. They rarely allow any 'stuff' to border them. They hardly get depressed and do not live their lives through others' values. They live a life in a state of feeling powerful without wishing to abuse others and in full control of themselves. They are full of fun and have respect for themselves as well as others.

In addition, try to always be in a jovial mood as children. What I mean by this is, make it a point of duty to be cheerful and friendly to people you meet, even those you meet for the first time. Remember, it takes only 17 muscles to smile but 43 muscles to frown—so smile as much as possible. This helped me a great deal, try it.

AN OPTIMIST, NOT A PESSIMIST

> "A pessimist sees difficulty in every opportunity; an optimist sees opportunity in every difficulty."
> Winston Churchill

The problem we have is that we usually 'see the glass half empty instead of half filled.' It is very good if we can see hard times as challenges instead of problems. It is very important to be optimistic in everything. It is only when you get to this stage in handling depression that you can grasp the idea that things change, because you will feel changes taking place already. However, we should know that we are not born depressed.

When you face a situation that is too dark for your comprehension, look around for there must be an antidote lying in wait for you. There is no challenge without a solution. Having this in mind causes happiness from the inside.

Here are some examples and solutions to them:

1) I am the only child

Being an only child is not a crime. There is a thousand and one only child today who lives happily. God made you the only child of your parents for a reason best known to Him. Do you know what would have happened, if you had siblings? After all, being the only child gives you the undivided attention of your parents, unlike others with siblings.

2) I don't have a job

It actually feels like hell without having a job. No one will say it is a good feeling—but when job is not forth coming we may need to step back and stop pushing for a while. May be in God's calendar, our date has not come. When we try to force change, the wrong time, we usually end up feeling dejected. The upside of this is to seize the opportunity to establish what we really want to do, rather than what we think we should do. There is this saying: 'Identify your obsession, make it your possession.'

3) I have no children

The Bible made us to understand that children are inheritance from God. I used to tell my friends that the relationship we have with God is the one of sheep and shepherd. He knows we are hungry, but will take us to the field at his own discretion.

Let us not forget that so many people are depressed today as a result of their children. So live happy knowing that your shepherd is aware that you need food.

4) I am not beautiful/ handsome

When I was much younger, I used to believe that some people are not really beautiful /handsome, but when I became an adult my ideology changed. I discovered that an artist designs his work the way he wants, so is our designer. I want to tell us that we are exactly the way our designer wants us to be. Relatively speaking, we all represent the true image of our creator's desire. IN FACT; NO ONE IS MORE BEAUTIFUL / HANDSOME.

5) I am overweight

There are millions of people who are overweight, but not depressed. The upside is that we have choices. Being overweight is often due to feeling depressed and having little self-respect. This might be because we have not given enough psychological nurturing to ourselves. We can turn this situation around by changing the message we give ourselves. We can take time out from trying to look better for other people and concentrate more on feeling better for ourselves.

6) Not married yet

Having a partner is a sweet experience, but shall we prefer to be married today and widowed tomorrow? I think none of us will like that. So to be on the safe side, let us wait for our own page to be opened—every human being has a page in that big book of creation. I have an aunty who was due for marriage when I was in primary school. But she got married when I finished my NYSC. Check out the number of years, but she is married now, that's all that matters.

Besides, being single gives us greater opportunity to help ourselves to grow up and finish our childhood. We can make good strides in taking advantage of not being in relationship. Many of us realize that sorting ourselves out works better when we are single, because we do not have to give to another and compromise ourselves.

7) People do not love me

People do love you; maybe you do not love people. I told my school mate that complained of not being greeted, to greet people. I advised him, 'since you want people to greet you and they fail, or did not recognize you—recognize them and then greet them. Remember, you do not have power to change the way people behave towards you, but you do have power to change your response to people. By the time you do unto others what you want them to do to you, it's only natural that they will reciprocate.

Responses to inferior thoughts (respond as if you are doing it for another person).

Thoughts	Responses
You're hopeless.	You are not hopeless, but only feeling down at the moment and will get better soonest.

You can do nothing right.	That is not true, you can do many things right.
You are an idiot.	You are not an idiot, but a normal human being with some challenges.
You are worthless.	No, you are not worthless, just that it is not yet time.
You are not good like your friend.	You are good in your area of assignment.
You are poor	You are not poor, because the only thing constant is change.
The society has used and dumped you	It is a lie, you have contributed your quota to the society, and gave way for another to do same. Besides, you have a thousand and one thing you can still do with your life.
Why bother, nobody cares.	God cares and I care.

You never get it right.	You get many things right.
Nobody loves you	I love you and God loves you.

Note: The above method is a guide to use in responding to whatever negative or inferior thoughts you are having.

CHAPTER FIVE

HOW TO HANDLE DEPRESSION: FOOD PLAN AND FITTNESS

> "The wise man should consider that health is the greatest of human blessings. Let food be your medicine." Hippocrates.

The bottom line is that good food helps our depressive mood. Evidence has shown that good food can provide huge benefits to our emotional wellbeing. Let us desist from eating junk food; this is the kind of food that offers short term comfort, but injects a longer-term set back. There are so many medical advices available on foods that have the ability to change our mood, our levels of alertness, anxiety, stress, composition in brain, etc. This is said to be because the nutrients in food are precursors to neurotransmitters, the chemical messengers that carry information from one nerve cell to the other. Also food is made up of different nutrients which help the body system.

Notwithstanding the theoretical function of food, we can roughly divide food into those that most affect depression and those that support recovery.

Affect depression	Support recovery
sugar, wheat, caffeine, alcohol, chocolate etc.	water, vegetables, fruits, oil-rich-fish, Fibres, protein,

Below is what food does to our body

- Protein can boost alertness; our mental ability. High protein food include: fish, poultry, meat, eggs, green vegetables, cheese, milk etc.

- Carbohydrates can help relax us and create an anti-stress effect. Research has shown that dieters tend to become depressed after two weeks into a diet due to decreased carbohydrate intake. Eating carbohydrate will trigger the release of insulin into the blood stream, which produces a sense of calm and after eating a large quantity, it induces sleep. Carbohydrates are whole-grain, bread, rice, paste, crackers, cereal and fruits.

- Caffeine: Evidence has shown that one or two cups of coffee a day can add a lift. It is an unusual stimulant in that it does not require more doses, day-by-day, to get the same effect. Any more than two cups a day can be counter-productive.

- Folic acid: Deficiencies have been linked to depression in clinical studies. Psychiatric patients were found to have a much lower level of folic acid than the general population. Just 200 micrograms was enough to relieve the symptoms of depression, which is obtainable from a portion of cooked spinach or a glass of orange juice.

- Selenium: A lack of selenium has been shown to cause bad mood. It causes anxiety, hostility and depression. The right amount can help us feel better and to get a daily dose, we need one Brazil nut, avocado pear etc.

My experience in all these, is that whenever I eat much of junk food I feel depressed, sluggish and worn out. But when I eat good diet, I feel lighter, more energetic and happy. Even though we eat much of carbohydrate in our society due to unforeseen reasons, we can still organize our diet to concentrate on health.

Remember:

- ❖ Eat five portions of fruits and vegetables a day.

- ❖ Eat three meals a day.

- ❖ Take plenty of water.

❖ Start your day with light food.

❖ Avoid eating late at night.

DO EXERCISE

> "True enjoyment comes from activity
> of the mind and exercise of the body;
> the two are united"
> Alexander Von Humboldt.

One of the most effective ways of changing our physical looks is to exercise. To accomplish this, it requires effort. When we exercise, endorphins are released into the body and this boost the mind and spirit. The problem we have in this part of the world is, we are too busy to exercise. We all have our eyes on money and how to get enough of it, thereby neglecting the maintenance and fitness of our body.

Many of us see exercise as work, and try as much as possible to do away with it. But we need to give our heart a work to produce the "feel good" endorphins that will occur as a result. If you are doing no exercise at the moment, then, a fast walk three times a week may be okay. Also, do press-up every morning as you wake up. If you have time, engage in morning jugging, it helps.

For those whose job do not give time except on Sundays, may visit gym centres near them early before other activities of the day. Many leisure centres now have well-equipped, reasonable priced gyms with quality staff to help plan an exercise routine for you. You can also acquire affordable gym equipment for personal use. If you are worried about how much exercise to start with, consult a doctor or a personal trainer. But if you are not comfortable in consulting anybody, try the ones I suggested or work-out the one that suits you. All that matters is to exercise.

ACUPUNCTURE

> "Acupuncture treatments have a calming effect and help those struggling with anger, hostility and frustration" Diana Fried.

In this book, we tried not to recommend the use of drugs in treatment of depression because of its addiction and other unclassified effects. But we recommend acupuncture because it does not involve the use of drugs, rather needles. This is inserting of needles into specific body points to improve health and wellbeing. Acupuncture is believed to stimulate the nervous system and cause the release of messenger molecules. The resulting biochemical changes influences the body homeostatic mechanism, thus, promoting physical and emotional wellbeing. We need this because when we feel depressed, we feel pains, aches in certain areas of our body which are symptoms of depression.

If you like this but do not know where or how to get it, ask any practitioner or doctor around he will direct you. When you go for acupuncture, tell the practitioner that you are depressed and you want treatment for that as well as your specific ailment. This will help the practitioner to plan the best treatment for you. One session a month is enough. Stop spending money on cigarette, alcohol or drugs when depressed. One session of acupuncture can change the way you feel than all the medications put together.

SPA TREATMENT

Spa treatment is giving soothing touches on the body which is generally called massage. It also involves a whirlpool bath which is one of the ways to reduce stress and body tics. The assignment of a spa centre involves elements which can help us relax and feel better. Going to spa entails being taken care of which is physically and culturally acceptable—we can carry on with the feeling of being cared for in a long while. 'physical contact is necessary to our well-being and even if the touching is from a stranger, if that stranger is a professional there to pamper you, that touch will have a beneficial effect' says Sadock.

Besides the care spa treatment can give you, precaution needs to be taken in getting a good, hygienic and therapeutic spa centre. This is because, many spa treatment centres which involve the use of whirlpool baths, very seldom do they change their water. They toss in some chlorine to keep bacteria counts down, but this does not eradicate organisms completely. So, take time to find a good spa centre, managed by a certified therapist. If not, go with your own water to be on the safe side or insist they change the water—please, to avoid adding insult to injury.

CHAPTER SIX

SPIRITUAL 'BACK-UP' IN HANDLING DEPRESSION

> "Some of the happiest people I know believe that there is all-powerful being to which they surrender their lives but, at the same time they are pragmatic." Alexandra Massey

Depression knows no bound. This means to say that a Christian, Pagan or Muslim can be irreparably affected by depression. Prayer is very good, but it should be a 'back-up.' If we follow the practical approach in the former chapters, back it up with prayers and references that are treated in this chapter, sky will be our spring board. FOR THOSE WHO BELIEVE IN GOD.

This suicidal feeling called depression has been for ages, so it will be good enough if we do not hide under the illusion that it does not exist amongst children of God. In fact, it is more with children of God.

> "Why art thou cast down, O my soul? and why art thou disquieted within me? hope in God: for I shall yet praise him . . . ' (Psalm 43:5 KJV)

The above quotation shows us that even David in all his riches and closeness to God had depression, but his hope was on God. That means he had performed the practical approach to depression, and then backed it up with prayers. This is seen where he said, '. . . for I will yet praise him' meaning when his approach works out, he will praise God. We cannot do this on our own that is why we need the 'back-up.'

Elijah was a powerful prophet of God, who God used to do mighty things, yet he was once depressed. Even with his entire prophetic prowess he was terrified and requested to die.

> ". . . and he requested for himself that he might die; and said, It is enough; now, O LORD, take away my life; for I am not better than my fathers." (1kings 19:4 KJV)

But there is this spectacular attitude these men of God—of old—displayed that we need to identify with. During their hard times, they still trust in God.

> "Though he slay me, yet will I trust: but I will maintain mine own ways before him" (Job 13:15 KJV)

In this contemporary world, many renowned men of God have suffered depression; some survived it, while others did not. This shows that it is not the level of your commitment in religion that exempts you, but your wisdom to handle it. God has given you wisdom; it is left for you to maximize it. A man of God by name, Charles Spurgeon had a terrifying experience of depression. This happened in his church, as a result of stampeding; many of his church members lost their lives. This left him depressed and he could not continue with his preaching that day. He was taken to the house of one of his deacons, where he stayed before he could recover.

A pastor that had his church in Ketu, Lagos was also a victim of depression. The church he spent money, devotion and sacrifices to build, was one time marked for demolition by the state government. This got him depressed, and in the cause of depression he had high blood pleasure. Later it developed into stroke, and he gave up the ghost. But the funny thing is that the church is still standing up till this day. He was a man of God, but he failed to apply practical approach in handling depression. Probably, he only prayed which was supposed to be a back-up. No wonder the Bible admonished:

> ". . . neither be thou foolish; why shouldest thou die before thy time?" (Ecc.7:17 KJV)

God's Calendar

> "For as the heavens are higher than the earth, so are my ways higher than your ways, and my thoughts than your thoughts" (Isaiah 55:9KJV)

In the midst of depression, let us remember that God has a different calendar from ours. He had pre-marked the date of every event. So bearing this in mind as children of God will help us to move forward. Let us not think that it is getting late based on our calendar, because that of God is different, and things happen based on His.

A woman has been childless for fifteen years since she got married. She did all she could to carry her own child, but all to no avail. However, her depression became hydra-headed in December, 2009 during the down-sizing of workers in the banking sector. This affected her, but little did she know that her date in God's calendar was at hand. The following year being 2010, she put to bed. So, my brothers and sisters, bear it in mind that God has His own calendar and everything happens based on that date.

Most times, people wonder why things have remained stagnant around them for so long. But the possible reason is that the day of favour has not come. When the day/date of favour comes, things will begin to change in positive succession.

71

> "Thou shalt arise, and have mercy upon Zion: for the time to favour her, yea, the set time, is come"
>
> (Psalm 102:13 KJV).

In every adversity lies opportunity.

> "In the middle of difficulty lies opportunity" Albert Einstein

It will be very rewarding if we can trust God in all totality. Believing that whatever situation we find ourselves in this life is for growth from God. One man was forced to leave Lagos state with his family when demolition of shops for road construction was announced. His shop was affected alongside the wife's. After a year he went to the village, his condition changed. He joined another business instead of the one he used to do in Lagos, and that was where his breakthrough came from. Right now he owns two cars, but had not even one throughout his stay in Lagos. So there lies opportunity in every adversity.

Believe in yourself

> "Faith is the strength by which a shattered world shall emerge into the light" Helen Keller.

Believing or having faith in ourselves is one of the best antidotes for challenges. We have powers we do not know exist until we put them to test. If we allow the natural progress to take place, our spirit will heal itself. That is, if we stop blocking the process of human healing, we will recover from any form of depression we suffer. If we can take away the tools we use to medicate ourselves, recovery will take place.

However, we have to allow ourselves to review our past: what we have lost. This experience will unravel the blockages that have been created. When we experience this two or three times we will realize that we can trust our inner self for restoration, because we will feel so much better for unburdening ourselves.

Ask God for 'neutral-thinking mind'

> "God grant me the serenity to accept things I cannot change, the courage to change things I can, and the wisdom to know the difference."
> Reinhold Niebuhr

Neutral-thinking mind can help us balance the way we see the world around us. It is about learning to accept events with a more impartial approach. With 'black and white thinking', we can often think that every event has happened just to try and get at us. But this is not reality. Asking God for neutral-thinking mind will help us not to view things from negative side but rationally.

The God-given mind will help us to start seeing events as clouds moving across the sky while we watch it go by. We don't get upset about what we cannot change, most especially those that have to do with destiny. This neutral mind will help us to let go of insatiable crave for material things: money, cars, property, cloths, fame, etc. The distraction we nurture and celebrate from all these, takes us far away from 'neutral thinking' and can keep us depressed.

Meditate on the word of God

Irrespective of the fact that meditation has been treated in the earlier chapter, there is still a need to treat this aspect of meditation in order to buttress the spiritual back-up in handling depression. To meditate on the word of God is to move the word from your head into your heart. This is making the word a permanent part of your life.

> "This book of the law shall not depart out of thy mouth; but thou shalt meditate therein day and night, that thou mayest observe to do according to all that is written therein: for then thou shalt make thy way prosperous and then thou shalt have good success."
> (Joshua 1:8 KJV)

From the above Bible passage, we can deduce that meditating on the word of God regularly will give us the privilege to enjoy the promises therein. This can be achieved by taking out some time to think upon a particular verse or passage with the intention of putting it into practice. As you do this, your mind will be open to Holy Spirit for His guidance. Through meditation, you can receive the secrets of breakthrough, success, peace of mind and happiness.

Word of God (For those that believe in Christ)

Bible is not silent about depression. Jesus also was aware of depression when He was on earth.

> "Peace I leave with you, my peace I give unto you: not as the world giveth, give I unto you. Let not your heart be troubled, neither let it be afraid." (John 14:27 KJV)

The above Bible passage shows us that, Jesus Christ is not oblivious of depression, but the upside is that He promised us peace after all.

> "… in me ye might have peace. In the world ye shall have tribulation: but be of good cheer; I have overcome the world." (John 16:33 KJV)

The above shows us that there must be tribulation and depression. So let us not abdicate our responsibilities; doing the practical thing and then back it up with prayers. We plan and ask God to determine our steps; we have aims and objectives but do not force the result.

> "In his heart a man plans his course,
> but the LORD determines his steps."
> (Proverbs 16:9 NIV)

Taking cognizance that God can take care of us is very important. Let us learn to take care of the fundamentals and leave the manifestations to God. Let us try as much as we can to give God a chance to perfect His work in our lives by allowing Him to search our lives. This is not my word, but the word of God as written in the Holy book.

> "Search me, O God, and know my heart: try me, and know my thoughts: And see if there be any wicked way in me, and lead me in the way everlasting."
> (Psalm 139: 23 & 24 KJV)

CHAPTER SEVEN

FOR THE CONCERNED

FOR THOSE THAT MEDICATE

> "If you do what you have always done, you will get what you have always gotten." Alcohol Anonymous

Without mincing words, cigarette, Indian hemp, marijuana, alcoholic drinks, class A or B drugs we take as a means to suppress depression does not add anything to our wellbeing. Many of us except novice, cannot practically deny that we do not know this, but we do them as a way out. Let me tell you point blank that depending on 'medication' to handle depression is lack of 'self-value.'

Examine it, and decide on which one to give up or cut down on, in order to have a better chance of recovery. If you cannot do it on your own, then seek for the assistance of Rehabilitation Homes, counsellors or medical institutions who can help you on this. Overcoming an addiction can pull so many into recovery from depression. So you need to clean up your medicating techniques enough to get closer to tackling the source of the pain.

The truth is that, withdrawing from these excesses can expose the depression which could be the reason that led to the addiction in the first place. But giving up on these will give you a better chance to handle depression in a practical way. If you are sceptical about this, you need to ask yourself this question: Do I really want to live happy? If the answer is yes, then, there are many ways to catch a fish. You can use the steps I gave in 'Road to Recovery' or make use of any counselling centre, institutions or hospitals who manage addiction. In terms of medical institutions, insist on professional and practical approach without anti-depressant drugs.

Be informed that medication is not only the use of substance or drug, thousand and one medicate with food, chocolate, soft drinks, ice cream, even work—anything to excess. Also, know that Satan always plant the thoughts to run to the shelter of these things in order to cushion the feelings of depression. But these thoughts inevitably lead to unrestrained life and an unrestrained life is doomed to destruction, BEWARE!

Side effects of medication

> ➤ It leads to addiction and dependency.

> ➤ Headaches with feeling of a tight band around the skull.

> ➤ Waking up so drowsy and groggy.

> ➢ Feeling like zombie from 6.am till noon with eyelids drooping and mouth yawning.

> ➢ Stomach ache and pains after meal.

> ➢ Weakness in legs so that walking becomes more like stumbling.

> ➢ Dryness of the mouth.

> ➢ Feeling dizzy and disoriented.

> ➢ Damping of the spirit so that one feels hardly alive.

FOR THOSE WHO LOST THEIR LOVED ONES

> "We cannot extricate death, but we can extricate fears. We must not demean life by standing in awe of death." Raphael

Losing a loved one causes depression. When we lose a loved one, we feel that the world has come to an end. We carry on with the impression that the demise of the person has taken the most essential part of us at the initial stage of the loss, but it fades as the days go by. That period is referred to as 'the beginning,' however, is a long one, and it doesn't end all at once. Its ending is more aptly described as 'slowly fading.'

After losing my friends, uncles, aunties and finally, my mom whom I loved so much, I felt horrible. I felt as if a slab sat on my chest. This is a normal human nature. But there are techniques I applied that helped to keep depression at bay. Below are the suggestions, try this, it will do you a lot of good; it worked for me and many others.

Surrender

The first wise thing to do is to surrender to the fact, that your loved one is dead. Accept the fate that she or he has been taken by the creator. I applied this in my own time by realizing that, the owner of the sheep has power to do with the sheep whatever he wishes. This means that he has the right to take it away for some other purposes at his own discretion. So God is the owner, and my mom the sheep—who am I to question what God does with His child? So, who are you to question what God does with your loved ones?

Shade Tears

The next thing to do is to shade tears for your loss. Do not hamper the flow of the tears in any way. Cry until your essence has had enough. Your mind will only expand what it deems safe to expand. Do not feel that people will term you to be weak—that is self-loathing. Cry as long as it takes, some may cry for hours, others couple of days, what is important is to let go of the grip, and allow tears to flow. You may even be surprise that you will not cry for long before getting back your life. By crying and shading tears, you release those feelings which are essential in handling depression; it is one of the fastest routes to recovery.

Take care of your emotions

During my time, I gave my mind the chance to rest from grief and just think of pleasant things as often as possible. I also tried to see only the positive side of things. Being with someone can help, and we can also find ways to bring joy to ourselves. Sometimes, doing the things we enjoy is very helpful: cheerful music, enjoying a morning or evening walk, spending time with little children, etc.

Focus on the future

Another good thing to do is to focus on the future. You need to remember you have a purpose in life and you have to accomplish your aim. Even your dead loved ones, if they can see you from where they are, will be happy that you are handling it well. You need to focus on the future in order to make your loved ones proud.

Eat well and exercise

Eating well and good exercise routine helps your mood a lot. Check out the topic on 'How To Handle Depression: Food Plan and Fitness' it will help you. Also, try and sleep well at least eight hours a day.

My advice to the grieving ones is to stay strong and sincere to their selves. You can use my suggestions or deal with it your own way, but please, do not use medication.

FOR POST-NATAL MOTHERS

Post-natal depression is not uncommon amongst nursing mothers. This is a depressive illness which affects ten to fifteen in every hundred women having babies, according to medical report. The feelings are not far-fetched, but the earlier you realise the symptoms the better to seek for help—it is never late. Talking to a therapist, friends and family relatives is a good help in this situation.

Some of the symptoms of post-natal depression include feeling of physically shattered, feeling isolated, low mood, feeling of having no admirers, feeling unwanted, lashing at partner, blaming everybody, etc. These and many other irksome feelings are identified with post-natal depression. But the upside is that, there are self-help suggestions below which can help you or anyone you know handle this.

- Be not afraid that you are depressed; many women experience post-natal depression and you will get better soonest.

- Talk to someone who understands and is ready to listen. This could be a doctor, your partner, friend or relative.

- Do not miss any good opportunity to sleep or rest during the day or night.

- Make sure you eat healthy food.

- Find time to do things you enjoy or that helps you relax: go for a walk, read magazine, watch movie, listen to music, etc.

- Locate any post-natal group around and share your feelings with them. Ask practitioners or nurses they will give you a clue.

- Ask others to assist you with shopping and other housework.

- Accept voluntary offers to assist you.

- Indulge in exercise routine—regular one can boost your mood.

- Make use of self-help books and websites.

- Contact organizations that support women with post-natal depression.

- Blame not your partner or relative—you need their support at this time, you know.

- Do not use alcohol or drugs to medicate, because it will only give you temporal relief.

Note: Some women who have severe illness need help from mental health services. This could be specialists' services for women with baby under a year old.

FOR TEENAGERS

Teenage age can be a very tough stage in our lives, and it is prevalent to feel sad or irritated every now and then. But when this feeling becomes intense that is when it is dangerous. The factor that triggers depression in teenagers is feeling of low-self-esteem. This is the stem that brings forth other depressive branches. At this stage, to make matters worse, we feel like no one understands us—but I do understand because I was once a victim, some of our elders do because they have crossed the bridge and many others, too. Also let me bring it to your notice that you do not need to feel this way anymore, because you have what it takes to feel better and happy. Below are some tips.

Inward look: The starting point in this exercise is to find out the things that make you feel low as a teenager and this can be actualized by looking inwardly, one does not lie to himself. When you identify it, tackle it.

Ask for help: When you identify your 'low spot' and find out you cannot handle it on your own, ask for help. The help could be from your parents, friends, relatives, mentor or counsellor; even a stranger can be of help.

Do not isolate yourself: Isolating yourself makes everything worse. Try as much as you can to socialize (though not easy but necessary). As you get out into the world, you will find yourself feeling better.

Do not use alcohol and drugs: At this time, you may be clouded with the impression that substance is the only way out but taking them for the purpose of suppressing depression will only worsen the situation. This leads to addiction, dependency and other unclassified outcome.

Stay natty: As the saying goes, cleanliness is next to Godliness. Make it a point of duty to always stay clean and neat; keep your surroundings natty. Keeping your things and environs neat evokes a special kind of sensation which is happiness, especially when it sparkles. You will never know this until you try it.

Eat well: A healthy man is a happy man. Good food boosts our mood. So eat well. Try and eat vegetables, it is very important. Also make sure you eat fruits every day. Read more on food plan in the earlier chapter.

Keep fit: Ever heard of 'runner's high?' You actually get endorphins rush from exercising, which makes you instantly happier. Exercise not just alone, but with friends or someone else.

FOR THOSE IN PRISON

> "Experience is not what happens to you; it is what you do with what happens to you." Aldus Huxley.

Speaking objectively, for anyone who landed or ended up in prison due to crime or substance abuse, there is always depression. Some people may disagree with me but it is the fact; there is no smoke without fire. I watched an interview of an ex-convict on television, and when the boy opened up what led him to the act, I realized that there is no limit to the damage depression can cause. Most of the young people these days develop destructive coping mechanisms for problem solving, anger, depression or conflict management—experimenting or binging on drugs. When this happens, in order to maintain the life style, they indulge in different kinds of crime that may land them in prison when caught.

My candid advice to you is, irrespective of your background, social status or class, you need to realize one thing—there is no problem without a solution. Yes, you were depressed which led to a habit, then the crime and finally conviction, but that is not the end for you. You should realize that this is an experience, and what you do with it matters. You need to know that God still loves and has an assignment for you. Do not give up. Accept the depression that is, 'surrender.' Accepting that you are depressed will help you to 'face reality', which is the right track to recovery. Do not be beaten by life. Do not feel that you have failed, because there is something God has left for you—your destiny. Just work on yourself with the suggestions: take care of the fundamental and leave the manifestation to God.

Follow the steps as stipulated hitherto, and back it up with prayers, you will see a new change.

Remember

❖ Incarceration does not mean you have been rejected by God or loved ones; rather it's just a way of reconciliation.

❖ Utilize the opportunity and learn from your mistakes for a happy life thereafter.

❖ It is never too late for a change, you can turn your life around and make it good—bearing in mind that God has plans for you.

FOR BATTERY

Battery is a domestic violence and can be described as a cause of physical harm; it also includes mental and emotional forms of domestic abuse—an off-shoot of depression. All the people who batter, one way or the other have the characteristics of depression. These characteristics include: low-self-esteem, extreme jealousy and possessiveness, domineering attitude, holding on to stereotyped roles and supremacy, hypersensitive, substance abuse and domestic violence to cope with stress.

Battery is an uncultured act that can be carried out by anybody; meaning that it is not identified with a particular race, class of people or gender; rather it is usually influenced by upbringing. It could be a lawyer, doctor, teacher, therapist, driver, mechanic, footballer, pastor, imam, etc. What a child sees his parents do, that, he grows up to do (children are good copiers).

The actions of those who indulge in battery are rooted in the psychodynamics of domestic violence patterns observed and learned in childhood. They lack the assertiveness needed to communicate in everyday relationships with other people, and resort to domination to maintain a sense of control over their immediate environment. They express at home what they are unable to express in public.

The question is, why do people batter? Most people who batter have been exposed to domestic violence as children. They are often victims of child abuse. They have watched their fathers abuse their mothers and have observed their mothers accept and endure it. They have learnt to express powerful emotions in destructive ways. They are driven by a need for dominance. As adults, they repeat the patterns learned in childhood.

However, there are ways to handle this aspect of depression. One of the ways is to realise that battery is a learned behaviour which can be unlearned, even though it's not easy. Education is the key to helping those who indulge in this nefarious act. There are counselling groups all-over, find a good one it will help you. Also, religious groups have counselling departments who will follow you up until you can control your emotions.

My advice for women whose friends or husbands appear to be depressed is to be empowered (be strong). Even though it may seem frightening, she must confront the man in a polite and subtle way: make him realise that she knows he is depressed. Put it this way: I think you are depressed and you need help. If he stonewalls, the next step is: Okay we have a problem and we need help.

The way you approach a man when depressed matters a lot, because it determines the kind of result you will get. If he accepts i.e. if he buys your idea, involve a counsellor, religious groups or his role model to help in counselling him and imbibe in him the implications of battery. This, my sister, will save you the beating. Note: desist from nagging a man when he is depressed.

FOR COUPLES

> "Keep your eyes wide open before marriage and half shut afterwards."
> Benjamin Franklin.

In this 21st century, we have many cases of couples who no longer take cognizance of fundamental reasons of the union (marriage), thereby causing depression for their selves as well as their children. Many couples have not physically divorced, but emotionally they have. This is a situation whereby a contribution or a suggestion from the partner is termed 'intruding.' They live separate lives, thereby putting the family under tension and pressure. Many are living with pains and guilt which transmutes into frustration and depression.

Irrespective of the fact that many homes are experiencing: depression, lack of peace, joy and happiness, there is still good news. The good news is, no matter what is going on today you can still enjoy peace in your home and save yourself the ugly experience of depression now or in near future. Is a matter of choice!

Below are some of the things to be considered in order to live happily.

Founder of marriage

You must know that God is the founder of marriage. He founded it with a principle that a man shall leave his father and mother and shall cleave to his wife as one flesh. This means that, couples should accept each other as one flesh. When Adam saw Eve, he said, 'This is the bone of my bones, and flesh of my flesh . . .' So, couples, stop seeing your partners as different bodies. Knowing that you are one is a good start that will enhance a happy life.

Understand your partner

One of the things that cause break-ups in marriages is lack of understanding of the partner and his or her temperament. Know your partner and work in agreement. Besides, marry your partner for 'who' he or she is and not 'what' he or she is. Note, do not marry out of pity. Marring out of pity leads to depression.

A price to pay

For every good thing in life, there is always a price to pay. The price in marriage is, find out the rules and regulations guiding marriage and carry it out. The rules involved in friendship are quite different from the one of marriage though they have things in common. The problem many couples have these days especially, the young ones is that, they see marriage as an extension of friendship. But, marriage is a union unlike friendship. So find the rules and play your part diligently.

Self-understanding of marriage

Self-understanding in marriage is very important. Understand the purpose why God sent you into that marriage. You need to understand that major purposes God sent you into the marriage are to make the life of your partner meaningful, joyful, peaceful, and above all fulfilled.

Effective communication

Effective communication is one of the things that extend the life span of marriage. So to utilise this and make a happy married life, your communication must be mutual. Talk to each other and share things together, even edifying jokes make love and marriage strong.

Try these suggestions; you will see how you keep depression at bay from your marriage and children.

CONFRONTATION

"Are you in earnest? Seize this very minute! Boldness has genius, power, and magic in it. Only engage, and then the mind grows heated. Begin and then the work will be completed."

John Anster.

In our individual lives, in our place of work, in school, in the market, etc. there are people who their behaviours are hampering our recovery from depression—these are the people regarded as 'who.' These are people we need to confront. To effectively do this, there should be a drawn-out list of those who we need to confront. We need to be cautious when we establish this list, because we must take into account how we have been exploited and how plausible it is.

What we mean by confronting is not to scold or exchange physical blows with the person in question, but to face the fact and sort it out in a serious, mature and well-cultured manner. This simply means to come out from where we have been hiding and face the fact.

Below are guiding questions to help us achieve this.

- Who needs to be confronted?

    This may look simple, but be discreet while writing them down.

- How are they to be confronted?

Be wise in choosing the method because what works for another may not work for you. Try and find out what works for you. I think calm discussion is okay.

■ When are they to be confronted?

Timing is very important, choose wisely.

■ Expectant results.

It is very important to envisage the result you want to get in the cause of the confrontation. Please let it be for positive change, and not to spite the person or get back at him or her.

Note: Before you do the above, please, try to identify exactly what you need to do: whether to confront someone, tackle your historic anger, or confront yourself by asking yourself what is it you are frightened to lose if you tackle the problem.

FOR BLAMERS

"The willingness to accept responsibility for one's own life is source from which self-respect springs" Joan Didion.

Hiding away from responsibilities fuels depression. The problem most of us have in this part of the world is that we blame others for everything that happens. We usually believe that people have influence over us; thereby our lives revolve around them. The kind of dependent we are to others makes us vulnerable to make comments like 'I can't live without him or her' or 'he or she made me do it.' That is why I said above that, before you confront anybody, be able to identify exactly what you need to do. As humans, we usually live in fantasy that plays itself out and we have played along with it. Doing away with some of the below ideology will help us.

1 Someone is responsible for the way I feel

Ask yourself this question: Is it possible for someone to get inside me and influence the way I feel? If you are objective in answering the question, you will find out that it is your responsibility. The effect words have on you is based on your own thinking and belief. No one can put you down without your permission.

2 Expecting unconditional love from others

This may keep us feeling depressed when we believe that someone else will love us 'no matter what.' Wake up; every adult relationship is based on a contract, whether written or unwritten. It is a game of give and take.

3   He/she made me do it.

Bear it in mind that as an adult, whatever you do, you do it in your own discretion. No one can force you, except in some rare cases when the person forcing you is breaking the law: blackmailing you or pointing a gun at you. Apart from these, no one has much power except you give in.

4   I can't live without him/her

Please, wake up from your slumber. Who told you, you can't live without him/her? Did you come to this world with somebody? Of course you can live without him or her for you to be independent. Stop hiding at the back of someone for comfort; learn to stand on your feet.

ANGER MANAGEMENT

> "The minute you settle for less than
> you deserve, you get even less than
> you settled for" Maureen Dowd.

Anger is the strong feeling we have when something bad or unfair happens to us. There is no human being living his/her natural life that does not feel angry one time or the other, but the way we manage it becomes the resultant effect. When anger is properly managed, it does not result to catastrophe. But when roughly managed, the effect becomes disastrous. This could result to loss of job, our home, our spouse, our children, our money, our health may be affected, our security and even our freedom, should law intervene. We should learn not to settle for the less.

Below are good ways to manage anger:

1) **Express your anger in a healthy way.**

> "I was angry with my friend—I told my wrath, my wrath did end . . ."
> William Blake

When you are angry, PLEASE, express that anger but in a healthy way. The healthy way is, do not speak at once; count from one to forty or seventy depending on the level of your anger, in your mind before you speak. By so doing, you have summoned the courage and the best diction for the situation. Be assertive but polite in your expression: avoid the use of abusive words; be in control of your emotions; hit the nail on the head.

2) **Walk out from the scene**

> "When anger rises, think of consequences" Confucius

When you have expressed your anger in assertive way and the situation seems to encompass statements that are uncalled-for, walk away from the scene by simply saying 'excuse me' as courtesy demands. By so doing, you will eschew controversial utterances that induce disaster.

3) Be indifferent to those who enjoy your anger

> "He who angers you conquers you"
> Elizabeth Kenny.

Some people enjoy seeing others angry, and they can go any length to see you angry. Try and recognize the agents of anger and pay no attention to their utterances. By being indifferent to their provocative utterances, they will be disappointed and will not bother you in future.

4) Value peace more than anger.

Taking peace of mind as utmost important treasure will help you manage anger. Try and imbibe in yourself peace-loving culture it will help you a lot. Sri Chinmoy, puts it this way: 'you may have every right to be angry with someone, but you know that by getting angry with him you will lose your precious peace of mind.'

5) Look kindly upon others.

> "There are two things a person should never be angry at, what they can help and what they cannot"
> Plato.

One of the good things to do is to see anger-arousers as a five-year-old baby. If you can think of other person as a helpless child, your compassion and forgiveness will come into play. For example, if your younger sister accidentally hurts you, you will not have the desire to retaliate, but take her too young to understand the effect. So apply this with others, you will see how good you will manage anger.

6) Neutral-thinking.

"Let us not look back in anger, or forward in fear, but around in awareness" James Thurber.

One of the most effective ways of managing anger is to be neutral-thinking. Do not see every word someone says to you as sarcastic. Also, do not be afraid or get angry at criticism, rather utilize it as an advice cum correction.

7) Be open to others.

"Anger is an open instinct to show people that something isn't right"
Raphael

Being open to others responses is a good way of managing anger. When you are angry with someone, may be a friend for behaving in a particular way and the person tries to explain, be open to his/her explanation. This is usually effective when the person starts with apologetic tone like: I didn't mean to hurt you by what I said. Also on your own, try to explain the cause of your anger like: I was angry because you are the last person I expect to talk to me that way. By opening up to your friend's explanation and explaining the cause of your anger, you will come to terms with your feeling.

8) **Meditation**.

From my experiences, I found out that peace comes from within. Practicing meditation regularly brings your inner peace to the fore. If you can have access to your inner peace, you will be able to utilize meditation during testing times. Read more on meditation in the earlier chapter.

Historic anger

> "Anger will disappear just as soon as thoughts of resentment are forgotten" Buddha.

Historic anger is in affiliation with the 'bottled up anger' treated in the earlier chapter, but for the purpose of this section, we shall simplify it. This is the anger that is not expressed when felt. Because it has not been expressed, it buries itself inside us. If we are depressed, it is clear enough to say that we have historic anger.

This type of anger is not far-fetched in our society today. Unnecessary outburst or abusive expression on the road is good example of this historic anger. The reason for some of the road rage we have today is that the person who is enraged has piled-up anger waiting for whom to explode on; if the victim is unlucky, he could be the person that triggers it. But the following questions can be used to address historic anger and live happily. Ask yourself and supply the answer.

Questions:

- What do I feel angry about?

- With whom do I feel angry in the past?

- Why do I feel angry?

- What has being angry added to the situation?

- What would have been the alternative means to the qualms?

Answer the questions above, and try to make it succinct; it is a good way to handle historic anger, because the answers will melt the ice block in your heart.

Note: Anger management is NOT A QUICK FIX! It requires sacrifice: time, efforts, discipline and practice to be able to achieve a positive result.

MANAGING CHILDREN WHEN DEPRESSED

Disciplining of children are most times done behind closed doors, which makes it more secluded to homes. But it is a sensitive issue, especially when we are depressed. Many parents/elders abuse children in all manners whenever they are depressed. In the cause of depression, we lose our self-control and it is likely to affect the children in ways we will probably regret. This is because abuse is not restricted to physical or mental violation, but neglecting and not being present. To effectively manage children when depressed, below are suggestions:

Discipline with prudence

Disciplining a child is one of the best values in African society, even globally. It is a way of correcting or guiding a child towards the right path. But the bottom line is let it be done with prudence. Children who do not receive good and quality discipline are always frightened. They are always anxious of getting punished, and to a large extent get things wrong. This creates fear and lack of confidence. So parents/elders, learn how to deal with children when depressed. You can use write-ups to pass on your instruction or any other palatable means, but PLEASE control your temperament when dealing with them.

Believe in them

Parents/elders should learn to believe in their children or younger ones. Please stop underestimating or neglecting them simply because they are not as good as their mates. All you need to do is to help and harness their areas of competence. There is no human being without a good side. Discover their strength and areas of calling, and then start on time to build them up. Send them to such places on a good day and when depressed.

Do not use foul language

Use of foul language when depressed is very common in our society. Using foul words on children when depressed is not good. Mind you, name-calling, lashing out, etc. are abuse—it does not help in building the image of a child; if it is possible for you not to comment on their behaviour when depressed, the best. Correct them when you have gotten your temper under control, in a mild and subtle way.

Allow them to play

When depressed, one of the best things to do is to allow the children to play outside with their mates. This to a large extent will give you chance and time to practice some suggestions and get back your life. Also, you will avoid exploding on them as a respite to your challenges.

A child needs care

It is pertinent to note that being depressed does not guarantee you abdicating your responsibilities on children. Remember, children always need care and support. If you are able to provide care for a child when depressed, it will be easier for you to pass through any huddle of depression. We must be aware that we approach children and younger ones the same way we approach ourselves.

FOR PLWHA, VENEREAL AND TERMINAL DISEASES

> "I know God will not give me anything I can't handle . . ."
> Mother Theresa

People living with HIV and AIDS, venereal and terminal diseases are often stigmatised in our society. These stigmas are often caused by fear, ignorance, denial, intolerance, misinformation etc. The stigma is of two categories: stigma people develop towards themselves and enacted stigma by others. Because of these stigmas, we feel unwanted, out of form, dejected and depressed.

My assertion is that you should know that you are fearfully and wonderfully made by God. In addition, He is not ignorant of your situation, He knows better than you do. Know it today, that having this venereal disease is not the end of your life—you still have wonderful life ahead of you. Know that you have this infection, but it is not going to kill you except your creator wants it so and we all must die someday. Do not carry any undue burden or quilt: choose not to live in the past or regret it, for you do not know what tomorrow holds. Love yourself the way you are, and be happy. Go out, mix up and enjoy yourself for it is your right to be happy. Below are your rights:

❖ Right to healthcare without discrimination.

❖ Right to speech and expression.

❖ Right to shelter.

❖ Right to adequate nutrition.

❖ Right to free movement.

❖ Right to life.

❖ Right to employment.

❖ Right to education.

❖ Right to security and safety.

❖ Right to freedom of worship.

❖ Right to vote and to be voted for.

- ❖ Right to family life.

- ❖ Right to dignity.

- ❖ Right to seek legal action if discriminated.

- ❖ Right to privacy—confidentiality.

Remember:

- To eat appropriate diet.

- To maintain a proper hygiene.

- To treat and manage opportunistic infections.

- To rest, it is very important.

- To avoid eating any raw or uncooked meat, poultry, fish or egg.

- To use anti-retroviral therapy (ART).

- To always go for check-up.

- To love yourself and others, this will help in reducing the spread of venereal diseases.

FOR FAMILY SUPPORT

> "Family . . . is a perpetual source of encouragement, advocacy, assurance, and emotional refuelling that empowers the child to venture with confidence . . ."
>
> Marianne E. Neifert.

African society used to be known with a superb support and respect for family members who have problems. But due to embracement of western culture the support for family members is headed to rock. Western culture has led to increasingly isolated nuclear families we have today in African Society, thereby causing a breakdown in our protective kinship structure. This may explain why a large proportion of subjects with depression have weak or no family support.

Most of the people who are depressed today, especially as a result of illness or incapacity find it difficult to heal due to lack of friends and family support. It is therefore important that the family support system is resuscitated to cater for the health of its members. Many stakeholders in the communities, such as religious and social groups may contribute to the support networks needed to strengthen the roles of family in promoting and protecting mental health of its members.

Investigations reported that 'the higher the levels of support provided by family members and friends, the less the stress due to disease leading to good outcome in secondary prevention and prognosis of depressed symptoms' (Internet Journal of Family Practice). In Africa generally and West Africa in particular, people are shielded from untoward effect of circumstances by support from families, friends and others.

Preventing Suicide

A suicidal person may not ask for help, but that does not mean help is not needed. Most people who commit suicide do not want to die—they just want to stop hurting. Suicide prevention starts by recognising the warning signs and taking it seriously. Warning signs are: mood swings, obvious changes in eating and sleeping habits, hopelessness, talking about killing or harming oneself, writing a lot about death, seeking out things that could be used in suicide attempt, such as weapons, drugs, etc. This is more dangerous if the person has a mood disorder such as depression, suffers alcoholic dependency, has previously attempted suicide, or has a family history of suicide.

If you think a friend or family member is considering suicide, you need to speak up to save a life. Speak up if you are concerned and seek for professional help immediately. Through understanding, reassurance, and support, you can help your loved one overcome thoughts of suicide.

What to say

- You are not alone in this, I am here for you

- You may not believe it, but your feeling will change.

- I may not understand exactly how you feel, but I care about you.

- You are important to me; your life is important to me.

- What can I do now to help you?

- Even though you feel this way, but I want you to know that there is a lasting solution to every problem.

Do not say

- It's all in your head; you have your life

- We all go through times like this.

- I can't do anything about your situation.

- What is wrong with you?

- You should be better by now?

Helping an addict to recover

Addiction is a disease on the addict as well as the owner—even more on the owner. What I mean by this is that the consequences of addiction, to a large extent affect friends, relatives and family members more than the victim. Igbo proverb says, 'whoever his brother has badly dancing steps bears the scratch.' So, most times the victim no longer cares because he or she is headed to destruction, but it is his or her people that bear the shame. That is why you need to use the suggestions given below to help the person.

Desist from enabling the addict: This means discouraging them from going on with their habits (support wise). But this is very critical and it requires wisdom, because at times you may think you are discouraging them unknown to you, you are actually fuelling the habit. Find out the best strategy and utilize it. Achieving this will make them face reality.

Do not deny them the consequences of their habit: It is good to allow the person to take responsibility of his or her action most times so that lessons would be learnt.

Direct them to treatment: When you see that the person is remorseful after the influence of addiction has left, then utilize the opportunity to direct the person to treatment.

Practice detachment: The idea behind detachment is that you can love the person, but hate their disease. Try and look at their outrageous behaviour as effect of their disease without taking it personal. Still love them though, but distance yourself from their behaviour. By so doing, they will begin to see reasons with you.

Do not react to their behaviour: Stop scolding at addicts when they are under the influence of their habit, because this worsens the matter. But talk to them in a good atmosphere, and when he stonewalls, do not insist, leave it for another moment.

Advice for family and friends

✓ Accept and respect depressed people around you for it will help them recover.

✓ Love and care for depressed people for it will give them assurance.

✓ Keep them company for it will give them hope.

✓ Assist them financially to meet their daily subsistence needs.

✓ Encourage them to talk on how they feel and be willing to listen without interruption.

✓ Encourage them to get help, like seeing counsellors.

✓ Encourage them to read good self-help books.

✓ Do not criticise or judge any depressed person around you, even though you might want to.

FOR THE GOVERNMENT

"The government is the potent omnipresent teacher. For good or ill it teaches the whole people by its example . . ." Justice L.D Brandeis

In order to handle depression effectively, all hands must be on deck. The government has a role to play in helping citizenry recover and prevent the negative outcome of depression. Research and monitoring areas need strengthening, especially in this part of the world. Data on drug use and abuse amongst youths these days are alarming. Data can be utilised for education and training purposes for professionals who have to work in this substance and drug abuse field. It can also be used for community education, justification of resource allocation and programme evaluation. In short, data can be used for planning, for prevention, care and evaluation. Research and monitoring data is part and parcel of social development agenda that is alive to efficiency and effectiveness.

With the government's full participation in helping its citizenry who are depressed, there will be the following:

- A comprehensive and integrated approach using different models and treatment intervention.

- There will be ensured policies aimed at reducing stigma and protecting the rights of people living with venereal diseases.

- Community-based organizations and other formations should be engaged in a collaborative working relationship, merge if necessary for relevant drug policies and resources.

- Government departments and units should create appropriate policy environment, subcontracting human and community-based agencies to deliver preventive and treatment programs.

- The organizational framework and personnel will be sensitive.

- Government should establish more of psychiatric hospitals, also train more man-power in psychiatric department.

- Government should also promote establishment of autonomous self-help groups/support groups.

- Government should give special 'intelligence security' training to young and unemployed graduates to help fight the insecurity. This will also help in reducing unemployment and depression that accompanies it.

CHAPTER EIGHT

DISCOVER YOUR 'COMFORT ZONE.'

"Now and then it is good to pause in our pursuit of happiness and just be happy" Guillaume Apollinaire.

I used this term 'comfort zone' to explain the things that tickle us or make us happy. It may be small, but the bottom line is that everybody has a 'comfort zone.' We all have something that fills us with joy, freedom and fun. The truth is that when we are depressed, we brush these things aside because of their smallish nature believing that doing it is a waste of time. But that is wrong, let us change this attitude and use the 'comfort zone' for our own good.

'Comfort zone' is what takes away curtain that prevents us to see outside the window. This is action that holds a line to the soul, our spirit, our essence and our child. It is the thing we do that puts the fun back into our lives. It is something that fulfils us like no other. We have to discover it and make sure we carry it out regularly. This could be anything but 'medicating' or immoral activity. Apart from these two, it could be anything like activities or games you played when you were a kid, adolescent or adult. Some of these may look funny or childish that you feel shy to engage in them again, but it does not matter. The point is that it makes you feel happy.

One of my friends once asked me: 'Raph! What is it with you and children?' I laughed and replied her, 'You will not understand.' She did not understand because that is my 'comfort zone.' I feel welcomed home whenever am playing with children, especially those below five years.

It could be a particular dancing step.

It could be a brand of music that accelerates you.

It could be a childish play that tickles you.

It could be watching acrobatic movement of the lamb.

It could be early morning or evening walk.

Discover yours and live happily.

Beware:

o   Beware of friends that keep you depressed and do away with them.

o   Beware of fake pastors, native doctors, spiritualists and imams that depress people from what they say.

o Beware that people have every right to treat you the way they want so long as they are not breaking the law.

o Beware that you have no power over other people's behaviour, but you do have power to change your response to others.

o Beware of people you compare yourself with.

o Beware that anyone can make a mistake, but fools practice mistake.

o Beware that death is inevitable and we all must submit to transition someday.

o Beware that old age is not a crime rather a blessing.

o Beware that lies cause unnecessary stress in your life and keeping vigilant to maintain the lies is demeaning.

o Beware that we all have different assignments in life.

o Beware that it is okay to take responsibilities for your actions.

o Beware it is not bad to be different from others.

o Beware it is okay to need other people in your life.

o Beware it is okay to say 'no' to things you do not want.

o Beware that the only thing constant is change.

o Beware of predestination.

o Beware that there is no problem without an antidote.

Conclusion

As you have read to this stage, it is now clear enough to you that so many things can cause depression in our lives and people handle them with different approaches. Experiencing depression is a part of human life, and no man in his right mind will deny that. There are three stages of experiences in life: the mountain top, the plain and the dark moment. The mountain top experience is when things are rosy; the plain experience is when things are just normal; while the dark moment is when things are tough. Any one you find yourself in, just know that things will definitely change—use the suggestions given in this book to move on. The enemy will use the third stage to dehumanize you which is the downside, but the upside is, no condition is permanent.

The suggestions given in this book are 100% practical. It has worked for many people in different situations. You are not under any obligation to try all, check for the ones suitable for your situation at the material moment and apply them. You are not expected to chronicle the suggestions before you can get a positive result—practicing two or three of the suggestions may be all you need to get back your life.

Bear it in mind that, any time our spirit is heavy or down-cast the enemy wants to steal our worth. But using the practical approach as suggested in this book will help us recover and eschew the enemy taking upper hand. As we recover, there will be no big ceremony to welcome us home. But we will only look back and realize what has changed. Gradually with God's help, we will learn to expect the best and get it. We will look back at things that used to demoralize us and will laugh, because of the practical approach without medication we dealt with depression: HOW WE HANDLED DEPRESSION AND LIVE HAPPILY.

WELCOME HOME

REFERENCES

Internet Journal of Family Practice, 2007—volume 5 number 2

Holy Bible, King James version by Thomas Nelson Inc

Manual for Training Peer Educators by UNICEF, 2003

Beat Depression by Alexandra Massey, 2004